1(es

About the Author

Shando Varda is a lifelong game-player who has taught and researched games for the last twenty years. In particular he has studied play in families and its many essential and enriching qualities.

As part of his research process, he has played with babies, children, teenagers, adults, and senior citizens. From this rich and enjoyable experience, he has come to see the role and value game playing brings to our everyday lives—whatever people's age.

He has two daughters and lives in Bristol, England.

SmartFun Books from Hunter House

101 Music Games for Children by Jerry Storms

101 More Music Games for Children by Jerry Storms

101 Dance Games for Children by Paul Rooyackers

101 More Dance Games for Children by Paul Rooyackers

101 Drama Games for Children by Paul Rooyackers

101 More Drama Games for Children by Paul Rooyackers

101 Movement Games for Children by Huberta Wiertsema

101 Language Games for Children by Paul Rooyackers

101 Improv Games for Children and Adults by Bob Bedore

Yoga Games for Children by Danielle Bersma and Marjoke Visscher

The Yoga Adventure for Children by Helen Purperhart

101 Life Skills Games for Children by Bernie Badegruber

101 Family Vacation Games by Shando Varda

101 More Life Skills Games for Children by Bernie Badegruber

101 Cool Pool Games for Children by Kim Rodomista

404 Deskside Activities for Energetic Kids by Barbara Davis, MS, MFA

Ordering

Trade bookstores in the U.S. and Canada please contact:

Publishers Group West
1700 Fourth St., Berkeley CA 94710
Phone: (800) 788-3123   Fax: (510) 528-3444

Hunter House books are available at bulk discounts for textbook course adoptions;
to qualifying community, health-care, and government organizations;
and for special promotions and fund-raising. For details please contact:

Special Sales Department
Hunter House Inc., PO Box 2914, Alameda CA 94501-0914
Phone: (510) 865-5282   Fax: (510) 865-4295
E-mail: ordering@hunterhouse.com

Individuals can order our books from most bookstores,
by calling **(800) 266-5592**, or from our website at
www.hunterhouse.com

1<u>0</u>1

Family Vacation Games

Have Fun while Traveling, Camping or Celebrating at Home

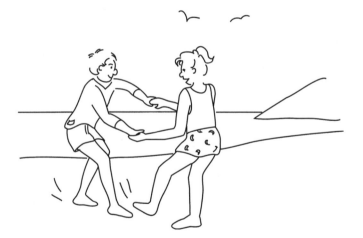

Shando Varda

Illustrations by Valerie James

A Hunter House SmartFun Book

Library of Congress Cataloging-in-Publication Data

Varda, Shando.
101 family vacation games : have fun while traveling, camping or celebrating at home / Shando Varda ; illustrations by Valerie James.— 1st ed.
p. cm.
Previously published under title: Family holiday games.
Summary: "Includes games new and old and from all around the world for parents to explore with their families and engage their children in a positive and fun-filled way. For families with children ages 4 and up"—Provided by publisher.
Includes index.
ISBN-13: 978-0-89793-462-6 (pbk.)
ISBN-10: 0-89793-462-8 (pbk.)
ISBN-13: 978-0-89793-466-4 (spiral bound)
ISBN-10: 0-89793-466-0 (spiral bound)
1. Family recreation.   2. Games for travelers.   I. Title: One hundred one vacation games.   II. Title: One hundred and one vacation games.
III. James, Valerie. IV. Varda, Shando. Family holiday games.   V. Title.
GV182.8.V37 2005
790.1'91—dc22   2005014038

Project Credits

Cover Design: Stefanie Gold   Senior Marketing Associate: Reina Santana
Book Production: John McKercher   Rights Coordinator: Candace Groskreutz
Illustrator: Valerie James   Customer Service Manager:
Copy Editor: Christy Steele   Christina Sverdrup
Proofreader: Herman Leung   Order Fulfillment: Washul Lakdhon
Acquisitions Editor: Jeanne Brondino   Administrator: Theresa Nelson
Editor: Alexandra Mummery   Computer Support: Peter Eichelberger
Publisher: Kiran S. Rana

Printed and Bound by Bang Printing, Brainerd, Minnesota

Manufactured in the United States of America

9 8 7 6 5 4 3 2 1   First U.S. Edition   07 08 09 10 11

Contents

Acknowledgments x

Preface. xi

Introduction

Why Play? 1

How to Use This Book 1

Playful Parenting. 3

Key to the Icons Used in the Games 3

The Games

Travel Games. 6

Games at the Vacation Destination 21

Beach Games 31

Sand Figures. 59

Outdoor Games. 66

Games to Play at Home 74

Birthday Party Games. 89

Games for Babies and Young Children 110

Appendix. 123

The Games Arranged by Specific Categories 130

*A detailed list of the games indicating appropriate group sizes
begins on the next page.*

List of Games

Page	Game	Pairs	Any size	One player	2 or more players	3 or more players	Large group
Travel Games							
7	The Farmer Went to Market		•				
8	Word Tennis	•					
9	Favorite Dream		•				
10	Airport Lounge		•				
11	Family Sing-Along		•				
12	Picture Storytelling		•				
13	Cat's Cradle	•					
16	Blind Distance		•				
17	Guess the Distance		•				
17	Road Snap		•				
18	Rock, Paper, Scissors	•					
19	I Spy				•		
20	Travel Trivia Quiz				•		
Games at the Vacation Destination							
22	Spoons						•
24	Broken Bottles	•					
26	Spoof					•	
27	Catch Me Out			•			
28	Waterfall		•				
29	Toe Fencing	•					
30	Yes, No	•					
30	One-Word Story				•		

Page	Game	Pairs	Any size	One player	2 or more players	3 or more players	Large group
	Beach Games						
33	Treasure Hunt		•				
34	Stepping Stones					•	
36	French Cricket					•	
37	Crabs				•		
38	Clock Tag					•	
39	Beach Burst-Out				•		
40	Any Changes?				•		
41	Moon Moon					•	
42	What Do I Hold?				•		
43	Hopscotch		•				
44	Long Jump		•				
45	Races				•		
47	Shadow Tag					•	
48	Rounders						•
50	Kite Frisbee		•				
51	Frisbee Golf				•		
52	Frisbee Tag					•	
53	Frisbee Boink				•		
54	Sand Dune Stalk					•	
55	One Pebble Game	•					
56	Pebble Golf				•		
57	Pebble Pictures		•				
58	Sand Maze		•				
	Sand Figures						
61	Jaws		•				
62	Seahorse		•				
63	Racing Car		•				
64	Mermaid		•				
65	Drip Castles		•				

Page	Game	Pairs	Any size	One player	2 or more players	3 or more players	Large group

Outdoor Games

Page	Game	Pairs	Any size	One player	2 or more players	3 or more players	Large group
67	Camera Kids	•					
69	Lost World		•				
71	Meet a Tree	•					
73	Duplication		•				

Games to Play at Home

Page	Game	Pairs	Any size	One player	2 or more players	3 or more players	Large group
75	Disc Jockey Hockey				•		
76	Racing Frogs				•		
77	Smaug's Jewels					•	
78	Sevens			•			
80	Flour Tower		•				
81	Pebble Breath Hold				•		
82	Sardines					•	
83	Snap					•	
84	Hunt the Slipper					•	
85	Kim's Game					•	
86	Ban the Word				•		
87	The Search for Alexander's Nose				•		
88	Pig				•		

Birthday Party Games

Page	Game	Pairs	Any size	One player	2 or more players	3 or more players	Large group
90	Charades					•	
91	Flying Fish				•		
92	Belly Laughs						•
93	Feather in the Air				•		
94	Penny Pinching				•		
95	Musical Chairs						•
96	Musical Statues					•	
97	Wink Murder						•
98	Chocolate Game					•	
99	Ring Game						•

Page	Game	Pairs	Any size	One player	2 or more players	3 or more players	Large group
100	In the Manner of the Word					•	
101	Balloon Burst					•	
102	Paper Drop				•		
103	Sketch Charades					•	
104	Guess Who				•		
105	Spoon Snatch	•					
106	Bone Game						•
109	Tip It						•

Games for Babies and Young Children

Page	Game	Pairs	Any size	One player	2 or more players	3 or more players	Large group
111	Play Wrestling	•					
113	Bear Hugs	•					
114	Flip-Overs	•					
114	Airplane Spin	•					
115	Whirligigs	•					
115	Pattycake				•		
116	Piggyback Rides	•					
116	This Little Piggy	•					
117	Knuckles	•					
117	Slip Slap	•					
118	Head over Heels			•			
118	Roly Poly		•				
119	Peek-a-Boo	•					
119	Touch My Nose	•					
120	Ceiling Touch	•					
121	Donkey Riding	•					
122	Walking Round the Garden	•					

Acknowledgments

I would like to acknowledge the inspiration I have received from the work of the New Games Foundation, Dale Le Fevre, and Joseph Cornell.

I would also like to acknowledge the game players of all ages from whom I have learned most of what I know.

Preface

Welcome to this book. These pages contain a treasure chest of ways to bring fun and laughter into family life.

Of all the things to do with children, playing with them is one of the most valuable and vital. Knowledge of games or access to them is essential to opening up the playful space inside each child. Games are like recipes. In cooking, people need to know the recipe in order to cook the dish. So it is with games, too—people need to know how the game works in order to play.

However, in this era of electronic media, many people, especially children, are spending large amounts of time staring at televisions and computers. This is part of modern life, but it is important to realize that when children are looking at screens, they are not having the vital experience of play.

As society becomes full of watchers instead of doers, people forget the many wonderful ways of playing with each other. Play increases social interaction and develops quality interpersonal relationships. Without play, people can become more isolated and may develop difficulties relating to others. Play strengthens bonds, releases tensions, creates greater awareness, and helps everyone in a family or social group to more fully understand and enjoy each other. The aim of *101 Family Vacation Games* is to reintroduce the many wonderful ways, old and new, of opening up the magic space of play. We call this "re-informing the folk subconscious." To do this, I have created this book to serve as an important resource. It includes a variety of games to create positive play experiences. People can explore the games, find the ones they enjoy, and create their own play repertoire with family or friends.

People who use the information in this book can personally discover the wonderful effects of play. They will become happier people who, in turn, will help to create a more playful world.

Enjoy the holiday time.

Best wishes,

Shando

For easy reading we have alternated use of the male and female pronouns. Of course, every "he" also includes "she," and vice versa.

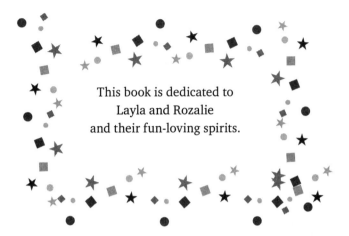

This book is dedicated to
Layla and Rozalie
and their fun-loving spirits.

Please note that the illustrations in this book are all outline drawings.
The fact that the pages are white does not imply that the people all have
white skin. This book is for people of all races and ethnic identities.
Complete political correctness is not always possible to achieve,
and I trust that the spirit of this book will shine through to all.

Introduction

Why Play?

When people play, no matter how young or how old they are, some great things happen. Barriers come down, trust develops, friendships are made, aggression is released, and most importantly of all, a wonderful positive energy runs through everyone involved.

Playing is even more important for children. A game is like a small world that helps them explore different parts of life. This is why children need to play different games at different ages. Play is how they experience and learn about the world and how it works. Through play, a child learns about trust, boundaries, taking turns, what hurts, what feels good, how to express their opinions, how to listen to others, and above all they learn that when they stick to their agreement about the rules of the game, they receive the wonderful reward of fun and laughter.

Teaching children to play will strengthen their coping abilities. They will flourish at school and be able to share games they have learned with other children. This, in turn, will help others and the school to function better.

Knowing a few games will also add another dimension to family life. Remember that culture consists of the things people actually do. Consider developing a family repertoire of favorite games. Playing these games will help all family members fondly recall previous good times as well as create new treasured memories. In a sense, participants will be creating their own family culture.

Laughter and fun contain a wonderfully invigorating current of life. There are many valuable, imaginative, and highly enjoyable ways to weave strands of play into family life. With the games in this book, people can unlock this sparkling positive force and let it flow through family life.

How to Use This Book
Role of the Leader

For a game to work, a basic agreement on the rules of the game has to be kept. When your children are young, you will have to act as the "leader" and remind them of the rules. As soon as they are able, encourage them to share in the "agreement of the game," and allow yourself to step back and simply become a fellow player. From time to time you will of course have to step back into the role of being in charge, but you will be pleasantly surprised at how quickly kids grasp how things work.

If you approach things this way you will help develop your child's own sense of fair play and self-regulation, which will have huge crossover benefits into other areas of the child's life. Children quickly develop a sense of fair play, which is why one of the worse things to be is a spoilsport. You will also find that your children become more self-reliant and able to cooperatively engage with other kids, as they will have learned this basic skill from you.

Obviously, to start with as parents you will have to take the lead in introducing the games. To do this you will need to choose games that fit your children's skill levels and abilities. When you introduce a game, get the rules across clearly and simply by explaining the boundaries and the use of any props. Often, having a practice run works very well. This demonstrates communication skills to your children, which they will then pick up on and use when playing with others.

Selecting the Games

Although the games in this book are well suited to people or families going on vacation, they can be easily adapted for many different situations and locations. Whether people are traveling or are staying at home, games are included to meet all needs.

The games in this book are organized into eight sections, each with a unique purpose: Travel Games, Games at the Vacation Destination, Beach Games, Sand Figures, Outdoor Games, Games to Play at Home, Birthday Party Games, and Games for Babies and Young Children. The games are grouped into a section by their main focus.

Even so, most games in this book can be used anywhere; the chapters are simply a suggestion. This means that some of the games might be applicable for several sections. For example, a game listed under Birthday Party Games could also be played at the park or beach. The games people choose to play will often depend on the occasion, number of people, and time constraints.

Each game in the book can stand alone. However, if you are hosting a birthday party or other special event, structure a play session by selecting several games from the different sections of this book. To do this, take into consideration the number of players who will be at the event and their ages. Also evaluate the amount of space and the materials available. The List of Games at the beginning of the book and the Games Arranged by Specific Categories at the back of the book are valuable tools to help find and choose appropriate games. Then, carefully plan the variety and order of the chosen games. Gather any needed materials and complete any needed preparation.

There are hundreds of ways to combine the games and use the ideas in this book. The goal is to keep the time fun. So be creative! Feel free to make family variations and improvements. Play is like cookery, and a game is like a recipe, delicious and nourishing—with fun as the end result instead of food!

Playful Parenting

Parents assume certain roles toward their children. While there is some compromise, traditionally and practically the parents have authority over the children. Although this role is natural, it often creates a struggle for power as the child moves toward independence.

One advantage of playing games is that parents can drop the parental role and interact with their children as players and equals. Both parent and child are bound by the common agreement and rules of the game. Something simple and very strong occurs when this happens. The child meets his parent as an equal and experiences the parent as a fellow player who has a right to respect and a turn at play. The child sees that, like him, the parent is also bound by the agreements made. This interaction adds a new dimension to parents' relationship with their children and helps to open the door to being friends, too.

Games can also be used to solve family disputes. For example, say an argument breaks out between children about who is going to wash the dishes after supper. Instead of choosing one child as the winner and the other as the loser, have a family discussion. Suggest the use of games to solve the argument. If everyone agrees, line up the complainants and select a game that they are all equally skilled at playing. Paper Drop (Game #79), Spoon Snatch (Game #82), and Rock, Paper, Scissors (Game #11) are good selections for solving disputes. The winner of the game gets to have her own way. There will be no complaints and no whining because every complainant has had an equal chance.

Key to the Icons Used in the Games

To help you find games suitable for a particular situation, the games are coded with symbols or icons. These icons tell you, at a glance, the following things about the game:

- The size of the group needed
- The level of difficulty
- If music is required
- If props are required
- If physical contact is or might be involved

These icons are explained in more detail below. Two icons included in other SmartFun books (age level and time) have been omitted here because the individual games can be easily modified to suit a variety of ages and because the duration of each game will vary depending on a number of factors, including the size of the group and whether or not the particular game appeals to the players.

The size of the group needed. There are games included for every size group, from individuals to pairs to those suited to large groups. If a game requires a large number of players, the game will be marked with the appropriate icon:

 = Requires an even number of players

 = Suitable for any size group

 = Suitable for one player

 = Suitable for 2 or more players

 = Suitable for 3 or more players

 = Suitable for a large group of 4 or more players

The level of difficulty. The games in this book range from those designed for beginners to more complex games that might be suited to older players. Games that are more suited to older players are marked with the following icon:

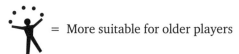 = More suitable for older players

If music is required. Only a few games in this book require recorded music. If the music is optional, it is noted as such; if it is required, the icon below is used:

 = Music required

If props are required. Many of the games require no special props. Though in some cases items such as balls, baseball bats, paper and pens, or other materials are integral to running and playing a game. Games requiring props are flagged with the icon below, and the necessary materials are listed under the Props heading. Note that optional props will also be flagged (except when optional background music is the only item listed).

  = Props needed

If physical contact is or might be involved. Although a certain amount of body contact might be acceptable in certain environments, the following icon has been inserted at the top of any games that might involve anything from a small amount of contact to minor collisions. You can decide in advance if the game is suitable for your participants and/or environment.

  = Physical contact likely

Travel Games

Traveling often requires spending a long time in a small space, which can be quite difficult for children. Keeping still is not something that comes easily to a child, so having some fun games planned makes for a more enjoyable and relaxing journey for everyone.

This section includes games that will occupy children while traveling. There are games for the imagination, such as Airport Lounge (Game #4), and storytelling games, such as Picture Storytelling (Game #6). The games will reveal interesting things about the children as well as adults! Some of the final stories will amaze and amuse the entire group.

The more games parents play with their children, the more game playing will become a tradition in your family. Certain games will become family favorites and be played over and over again by popular demand. In fact, playing games can help create a family culture.

Things to Bring
- Paper, pens, pencils
- Strings for Cat's Cradle (Game #7)
- Questions for Travel Trivia Quiz (Game #13)

The Farmer Went to Market

How to Play: One player begins the game by saying, "The Farmer went to market and took with him a ____." The player then fills in the blank with an object of his choice, such as a "cow." The object does not have to be something from a farm. It can be anything from a piece of string to a video to a space rocket to a newspaper, etc.

The player sitting to the left repeats what the first has said and adds another object. For example, "The farmer went to market and took with him a cow and a rooster." The third player in line repeats player two's statement and adds a new item to the list. Players take turns repeating what has been said and adding something new.

Of course, the longer the list, the harder it becomes to remember. A player who gets the list wrong is eliminated from the game. Play continues until there is one person left.

Variation: You can personalize the game by switching the farmer with another character and the market with another place. Players can add extra smiles by using characters from their own families. For example, "Aunt Sandra went to France, and she took with her a...."

Word Tennis

How to Play: The group is divided into pairs or teams, depending on the number of players. One player chooses a general subject, such as fruit. The other player or team says the name of a specific kind of fruit, such as "banana." Then the first player or team has five seconds to reply with the name of another fruit. No repeats are allowed.

Players continue taking turns until one side cannot think of a new item. The other side is then the winner of that round. The winner chooses the subject of the next round.

Examples
- Animals
- Famous singers
- Kinds of trees
- Cartoon characters
- Girls' or boys' names
- Vegetables

Favorite Dream

How to Play: Players think about their favorite dreams. The dream should be something concrete, such as traveling to Australia. Each player then writes a sentence about their dream. They should keep this sentence a secret from the other players.

One player starts the game. The other players try to guess his dream by taking turns asking him questions to find out what his dream is. He can answer only "Yes" or "No" to the questions asked.

The other players get only a certain number of incorrect questions. The leader determines this number, between ten or twenty, before play begins. Players who think they know what the dream is can guess, but they are only allowed three guesses. If the players reach the predetermined number of incorrect questions or if they run out of guesses, the first player wins the round. If the players guess the dream correctly, they win.

Examples
- Riding an elephant through town
- Playing soccer in the Olympics
- Meeting a famous person
- Eating an ice cream cone while sliding down a slide
- Swimming with dolphins

Airport Lounge

How to Play: Players pretend they are sitting in an airport waiting for their planes. The planes are delayed by fog, so all the passengers talk to each other and ask each other questions. Since the person being asked the question has no idea what it will be, they have to make up the answer on the spot. It is as much a surprise to them as to everyone else to discover who "they are."

Each person should answer at least ten questions. This gives the character a chance to grow and then relax as the spotlight falls on the next person. As the questions are answered, the characters emerge as if by magic.

The leader decides when the game will end. Then, the fog lifts, the planes arrive, and all the characters say goodbye to each other and catch their planes.

Examples

- What is your name?
- What country are you from?
- Where are you going?
- How old are you?
- What is the weather like where you live?
- What kind of work do you do?

Variation: If preferred, this imagination game can take place in the lounges of train or bus stations.

Note: This game can be played with many people taking turns at once or focused on one person at a time. Having one person the focus of the questions gives the game and characters more of a chance to develop and to be remembered!

Family Sing-Along

How to Play: The adults start the sing-along. They may enjoy remembering songs their parents used to sing to them. Singing these songs as adults for their own kids is one way to pass tradition to the next generation, helping develop a real family culture. These old songs will get the sing-along started and may create some laughs as the family tries to remember the words.

Next, the children take a turn choosing and singing a song. For example, the kids will most likely know songs from films and the radio. Then, the adults take another turn picking a song. Singing continues in this manner so that the whole family hears and learns each other's songs.

The length of time spent singing and the songs sung will depend on each family's preferences.

Notes

- It's important to foster a welcoming atmosphere for singers of every ability. It doesn't matter if a person forgets verses or simply stops singing. An accepting environment will help singers feel confident and help them to sing better.
- For song ideas, check out the Sing-Along section in the Appendix (page 123).

Picture Storytelling

How to Play: One player begins making up a story. When she gets to an interesting point, she stops. Then, the next player takes over and develops more of the story.

Players can add new characters, events, places, or themes if they wish. It helps not to get too fantastic too quickly.

Play continues until each person has had a chance to contribute to the story. This helps players to see that it is actually more fun to develop the story and hand it to the next person rather than create wild narrative tangents. The last player ends the story.

As children become familiar with the game, the leader may add additional rounds. That way, the stories will become longer and more complex.

Examples

- A road
- A lake
- A bell
- A fish
- A jewel

Notes

- This game requires a knowledge of basic narrative structure to help weave the storyline and to assist in bringing it to completion. Before beginning the game, it will be helpful to briefly talk about what a story is and the parts that make up a story. Have players to think about their favorite stories. Then ask them what elements made it such a good story. Ask them to keep these facts about stories in mind when playing the game.
- Before the game starts, the leader can help the players decide which things will appear in the story. This can help stimulate ideas and keep things on track.
- The imagination is a real mental muscle. Children will often relax into a quiet sleepy state after the game and "digest" the story. It's a bit like a meal!

Travel Games

Cat's Cradle

Props: String (thin, white parcel string is best)

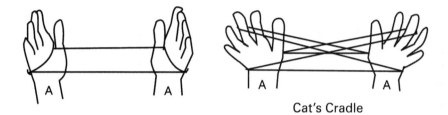

Cat's Cradle

How to Play:

1. Player A loops string around hands.
2. Player A hooks string from palm of left hand onto the middle finger of the right hand and from palm of right hand onto the middle finger of the left hand, making a...Cat's Cradle!

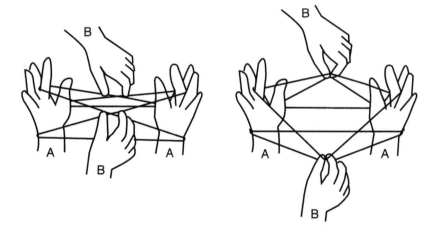

3. Player B pinches crossed strings between index fingers and thumbs.
4. Player B pulls the strings outward and down and up through the center gap, lifting the strings off Player A's onto her own and this forms...the Bed.

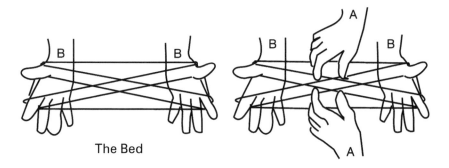

The Bed

5. Player A pinches the crossed strings between index fingers and thumbs
6. Player A pulls outward, then down and up through the center gap, lifting the string off Player B's hands and onto her own, making...Tramlines.

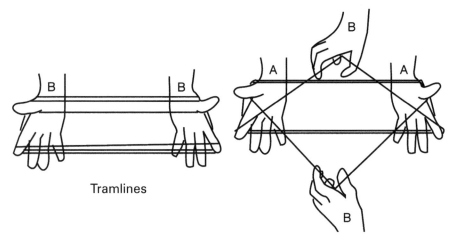

Tramlines

7. Player B hooks left little finger around right middle string and right little finger around left middle string.
8. They pull out, then down and up through the center gap, forming...the Manger.

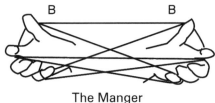

The Manger

9. Player A then pinches the crossed strings between her index fingers and thumbs. She pulls outward and up and down through the center gap, lifting the string off Player B's hands onto her own, making another Bed. Player B then pinches the crossed strings, pulls out, then down and up through the center gap, which creates an…Envelope.

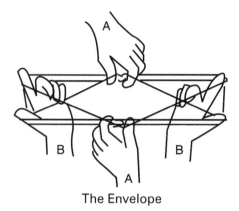

The Envelope

10. Player A then pinches the crossed strings at the edges of the Envelope, moves her thumbs and index fingers down, then up through the center gap, lifting the strings onto her hands.
11. If one of the players pulls the strings, she creates a…Fish on a Dish.

Fish on a Dish

Notes

- String games are played in all cultures around the world. This popular game probably originated in Asia.
- Always keep a piece of string in the car for this game. Thin, white parcel string works well. It is better to keep the string a bit slack than a bit tight.

8

Blind Distance

How to Play: The driver chooses an object far in the distance and announces the chosen object. Next, all the players close their eyes.

The players wait until they feel the car has reached the object. At that time, each player will call out, "Now!" Then, she will open her eyes. She does not say whether or not the car has actually arrived at the object. This way, the other players can still guess. When all players have had a turn guessing and have opened their eyes, the driver decides who the winner is.

Play resumes with either the driver or the winner of the last round choosing a new object.

Examples

- Bridge
- Church steeple
- Lake
- Hill
- Billboard
- Building

Note: Of course, the driver DOES NOT close his eyes!

Guess the Distance

How to Play: The driver chooses an object in the distance, starting with objects not more than one mile away. Next, all the players guess how many miles away it is. The driver then checks the odometer.

When the car reaches the object, the driver announces the mileage. The player who guessed closest to the actual number of miles is the winner.

Notes

- Keep your attention on the road when checking the odometer.
- This game teaches a sense of distance and how long a mile is.

Road Snap

How to Play: The leader decides on an object that the players are likely to see along the road. Everyone keeps a lookout for the chosen object. The first player to see the object calls, "Road Snap!" That player is the winner and chooses the next object.

Examples

- A tractor
- A bridge
- A woman with a stroller
- A bus stop
- A red car
- A cow, bird, or other kind of animal

Rock, Paper, Scissors

How to Play: Before beginning the game, players need to know how to make three signs with their hand. To make the rock, a player forms a fist. To make paper, a player holds out her hand, keeping it flat. To make the scissors, a player stretches out his index and middle finger sideways in a V shape to form "scissor blades" and curls his remaining fingers to his palm.

Explain the rules of the game. Scissors cuts Paper and wins; Paper covers Rock and wins; Rock breaks Scissors and wins.

Players divide into pairs. The players slowly say, "Rock, Paper, Scissors—shoot!" Players can either hold their fists behind their backs or gently bang them on something in time with each other, but they need to quickly make one of the three signs at the same time as they say "shoot." It is important that both players make their sign at the same time so that neither one sees what signs the other player has chosen.

The game is played over and over again. The fun is in trying to outguess the other player. Players can keep score or just play really fast and watch the patterns emerge.

Variation: Players in pairs may choose to enact the signs. If one has made the sign for Scissors and the other Paper, then Scissors is the winner. She may pretend to cut the "Paper" with her "Scissors."

If one has made the sign for Paper and the other the sign for Rock, then Paper is the winner. He may pretend to cover the "Rock" with his "Paper."

If one has signed Rock and the other Scissors, then Rock is the winner. She may pretend to break the Scissors by gently knocking her "Rock" against the "Scissors."

I Spy

How to Play: The first player chooses an object that he can see, without telling the others what it is. He then says the immortal words, "I Spy With My Little Eye something beginning with...." He then says the first letter of the name of the object. For example, if the chosen object were a flower, he would say, "F."

The other players then look around them and guess objects that begin with that letter. When someone guesses correctly, that player takes over as I Spy and chooses the next object.

Variation: Use colors instead of letters to include small children who cannot spell.

Note: This is an all-time favorite game among many generations. It works great in the car or in any situation.

Travel Trivia Quiz

Props: Trivia questions written on slips of paper

How to Play: The leader writes trivia questions on pieces of paper before the journey. She can ask different family members to contribute questions. During a lull in the journey, the leader asks players the trivia questions.

Examples

1. Add the numbers on the car license plate and divide by two.
2. How many aunts and uncles are there in your family?
3. How many miles is it to the next destination?
4. What color will the next taxicab be?
5. What do all of the ages of the people in the car add up to? (no asking individual ages allowed)
6. How many miles is it to the next bus stop?
7. How many toes are there in the car?
8. How many fingers are there in the car?
9. What is Grandma's favorite TV program?

Notes

- This game helps the family work together. They plan their activities before they travel, and this develops a sense of anticipation before the journey.
- Consider awarding prizes for different categories. Categories could be the most correct answers, most wrong answers, funniest answers, quickest, slowest, etc.

Games at the Vacation Destination

The holiday destination offers a new environment for the family to explore. There are many different landscapes to use in a playful manner, including natural features.

This section contains games that will work well in most types of surroundings. There are games to play on grass or against walls. Also included are games to play in nature and games to play while relaxing in the evening.

Spoons

Props: Playing cards; tea spoons or small stones or coins

How to Play: Players sit around a table and put the spoons in the middle of it. There should be one less spoon than the number of players.

For example, say there are six players and five spoons. Deal six piles of cards of the same number. Each number pile contains cards from all the four suits (hearts, spades, diamonds, and clubs). For example, there may be six piles that contain four aces, four kings, four queens, four jacks, four tens, and four nines. Shuffle these cards well, and deal four cards to each player.

The aim of the game is to collect four cards of the same type, e.g., four jacks. The players look at their cards and decide which cards they are going to collect.

Each player then decides which card to discard. He puts the discard down on the table to his left, keeping his hand on it.

When everyone is ready, someone says, "Pass." Each player slides her give-away card to the player on her left. She lets go of it and picks up the card that has just been passed to her. It is important that everyone does this in step so that no one gets to look at his new card before the others. This is especially important in the latter stages of the game.

If the card is the one she wants, she can keep it, or she can pass it or another card in the next round. The game proceeds with players passing and receiving cards. It is important that players pass the cards quickly. When players have practiced passing the cards, they can play really fast!

The game continues until one player gets four of the same kind of card. That person then takes a "spoon." When the others see someone go for a "spoon," they must all try to grab one as well. The last one to grab gets thin air instead of a spoon and is eliminated from the game.

For the next round, remove one spoon and one set of cards from the deck. Shuffle and deal the cards. Play proceeds as it did during the previous round.

The game continues until two players are left playing for one spoon. The winner is the one who gets the spoon.

Note: The player who gets four cards should try sneaking the spoon so that the others don't notice at first.

Broken Bottles

Props: A ball

How to Play: Two players stand at a distance from each other. The distance they choose is up to them. It will vary depending on their age, ability, and confidence to throw and catch the ball.

The players now start throwing the ball backward and forward between them. If a player drops the ball, there is a penalty. The penalties are:

1st drop: one knee
2nd drop: two knees
3rd drop: two knees, one hand
4th drop: two knees, one hand, one eye closed
5th drop: two knees, one hand, both eyes closed!
6th drop: you lose.

On the first drop, the player goes down on one knee and throws the ball back. If he catches the ball on the next throw, he may stand up. If he drops it, he must go down on two knees.

Each time a player drops the ball, the skill level needed increases. Yet each time a player catches the ball, the player is rewarded with an easier skill level.

For example, a player who has dropped the ball three times in a row is on two knees and using one hand. If she catches the ball, she would then be on two knees and using two hands. If she catches the ball again, she would then be on one knee. If she catches the ball yet again, she would be able to stand up. Each time she drops the ball, she goes back one stage.

This system of penalties and rewards gets players really focused on catching the ball.

Note: This is a ball-catching game between two players. To play this game, a child needs some catching ability. Play becomes harder as mistakes are made, and this can be discouraging.

Games at the Vacation Destination

Spoof

Props: Some small objects, such as toothpicks or buttons

How to play: Players hide their hands behind their backs or under the table. Place a different number of small objects in each player's hand. Players close their fists around the objects.

Next, the players hold out their fists. They take turns guessing how many objects are hidden in all the fists put together. No two players may guess the same number. The first player to guess can pick any number, but the last player to guess has the advantage of hearing other peoples guesses. After everyone has guessed, the players open their fists and count the objects. The player who guesses correctly or is the nearest to the correct number wins the round.

Note: This game helps players develop the skill of deduction because they use the other players' guesses to deduce what number of objects the others might be holding.

Catch Me Out

Props: A ball that bounces

How to Play: The player stands in a place with enough space to complete the movements required in each step. The player then progresses through the steps listed below:

> 1st step: The player throws the ball up in the air and catches it in both hands.
>
> 2nd step: The player throws the ball up in the air and lets the ball bounce once, then catches it in both hands.
>
> 3rd step: The player throws the ball up in the air and catches it in one hand.
>
> 4th step: The player throws the ball up in the air and lets it bounce, then catches the ball with one hand.
>
> 5th step: The player throws the ball up in the air, then claps his hands behind his back before catching it in both hands.
>
> 6th step: The player throws the ball up in the air, then claps her hands behind her back before catching the ball with one hand.
>
> 7th step: The player throws the ball up in the air, then claps his hands behind his back, then claps them in front of him, then catches the ball with both hands.

Variation: Change the steps to make the game more interesting. The complexity of the actions making up each step will depend on the age and skill level of the player. Some ideas for changing the steps include: jumping jacks, spinning once or twice, doing the splits, doing a handstand, kicking, and so on.

Note: This game for individuals encourages a child to complete a simple process that repeats itself with a bit more difficulty each time. The child learns how to focus and to master the skill in question by overcoming difficulties.

Waterfall

Props: A ball that bounces

How to Play: The first player throws a ball high in the air and catches it. This action is called completing the waterfall. When the player can do the waterfall, he then repeats it, making it more difficult by adding "rocks." Rocks are actions that must be done between throwing the ball up and catching it. Players must complete a waterfall for each "rock."

Rock 1: Touch your shoulders.
Rock 2: Touch your elbows.
Rock 3: Touch your knees.
Rock 4: Touch the ground.
Rock 5: Turn completely around.

When a player succeeds in "waterfalling" with rock 5, she has successfully shot the rapids. She may do a dance of triumph and give a loud victory shout. The next player takes a turn. Play continues until all players have had turns.

Toe Fencing

How to Play: The group divides into pairs, and each pair of players holds hands. Then each player tries to gently tap the top of the other player's feet or toes with her own. The round ends when one player has successfully tapped the other player's toes. Play continues for a predetermined number of rounds or until the players are tired.

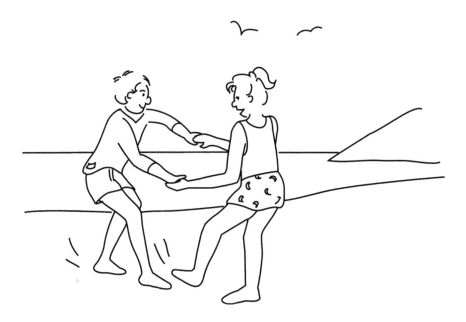

Note: The players should try to tap the other person's foot, not stomp on it!

Yes, No

How to Play: One player starts the game by choosing a common word like "yes" or "no." He then rapidly asks another player simple questions, which she must answer at once. He continues to ask her questions until she says the chosen word. When this happens, she takes a turn choosing a new, simple word. Then she asks him questions until she gets him to say the chosen word. Play continues in this way for a predetermined number of rounds or until players are exhausted!

One-Word Story

How to Play: The first player says a word. The next player adds another word. Players, in turn, say one word after the player before them. The only rule is that each word added has to make sense with what went before. This way, the words should form sentences.

Play continues in this way. The story grows sentence by sentence. There is absolutely no telling where the group's story will end up. The more spontaneous the contribution is, the better.

Notes

- In this game, players create a group story. Stories can be as fun, crazy, or complex as the players want them to be. Encourage everyone to be creative!
- Small is beautiful. Consider limiting players to five or ten sentences to start, which will produce mini vignettes.

Beach Games

Many family vacations often involve spending some time at the beach. It is a wonderful environment with fun features to explore. It is also a good place to play, and the games in this section help to make the most of the landscape.

This section includes games especially designed for a sandy beach environment. There are both action games and some slower ones. Also, the creative games featured will captivate the children's interest. If the environment is safe enough, there are games that encourage the kids to wander and explore for themselves. Children love to show what they have done or found. It is really important to them. If they know that someone will come and look, it encourages them to do things by themselves (for example, Game #43: Pebble Pictures).

Before the kids play at the beach, address important safety considerations. Protect children's skin with waterproof sunblock lotion. If necessary, choose the appropriate floating or life-saving devices according to the children's ages and swimming skills, and be aware of the potential dangers of any water toys, such as inflatable tubes, which can tip a child over. Please review water safety rules with each child. If there is no lifeguard on duty, always supervise children when they are in the water. **Never** leave them alone. It takes only a few seconds for even the most experienced swimmer to encounter an in-water emergency that requires adult assistance. Identify landscape features that might be dangerous, such as slippery rocks, and establish boundaries (places where children are not allowed to go). Also, make sure the children take breaks from playing to hydrate themselves by drinking plenty of liquids.

Things to Bring

- A football
- Soft balls (e.g., tennis balls)
- A hard ball
- A small baseball or whiffleball bat
- Buckets and shovels and a small rake
- A big plastic shovel
- Kites
- Frisbees

Treasure Hunt

Props: A list of items commonly found on a beach

How to Play: Make a list of things to find on the beach. Consider the location and perhaps limit how far away the players can go (within shouting distance works well). Stress safety, and tell them to keep away from hazards, such as strong currents or loose rocks.

Show the list to each player. The players then go and search for the objects on the list. The first one back with all the items is the winner.

This game is also fun to do in conjunction with a supervised group walk along the beach. The walk option allows players to safely visit different areas where they are more likely to find different objects.

Variation: Putting a time limit on the search helps to keep the children in touch as they will be all keeping an eye on each other to make sure no one takes extra time.

Examples
- Three shells
- A Popsicle stick
- A piece of seaweed
- A red pebble
- Something that is yellow
- The strangest pebble
- A stone that looks like an egg
- Shells that are white

3 or more

Beach Games

Stepping Stones

Props: A pebble or other small object

How to Play: Draw seven or eight lines in the sand that are about two feet apart from each other. Players take places along the first line. One player is the hider. The hider holds a pebble or small shell in one hand and stands at the last line. He puts his hands behind his back and hides the pebble in one of them. He then brings his hands out in front and moves his hands up and down, alternately saying, "Up and Down, Up and Down, the mermaid she went to town." It is good to say this quickly with rhythm. He then stops moving his hands with one in the Up position and one in the Down position.

The other players then each have to guess which hand is hiding the pebble. Is it Up? Or is it Down? Each player says his or her guess out loud. The hider then opens his hands and shows the pebble.

Players who answered correctly step forward one line. Players who answered incorrectly stand still. The hider then hides the pebble again. Play continues until one player reaches the hider. This player is the winner and then becomes the new hider.

Variation: Try players moving back one line if they get the answer wrong, though this slows the replacement of the hider.

Note: This is a seaside variation of the playground game. Players can personalize it as they wish. For example, the group may decide that the hider must wear seaweed hair.

French Cricket

Props: A baseball bat; a tennis ball or rubber ball

How to Play: One player is the first batter and receives the bat. The ball goes to the player who is the first thrower. The remaining players spread out around the thrower and the batter.

The aim of the game is to try and throw the ball so that it hits the batter's legs below the knee. So, the thrower tosses the ball at the batter, trying to hit him below his knees. The batter tries to hit the ball away with the bat.

The batter may not move his feet. So if he chooses to try to hit the ball behind him, he'll have to twist around while he's swinging in a way that allows him to defend his legs, which of course makes things more difficult. It is a good way to handicap older players, but if the players are young children, this rule can be waived. Players take turns throwing the ball at the batter. They try to catch any ball hit by the batter. Play continues until a hit is scored on the batter's legs or until a player catches the ball. The player who caught the ball or scored the hit on the legs then becomes the new batter.

Crabs

How to Play: Players sit down on the sand. They should arch their bodies backward, placing their hands down on the sand next to their head. Next, have them lift their behinds off the ground. Their hands and feet now support their weight. They are now "crabs." The new crabs practice moving around. After practicing, the game begins.

The players chase each other. They try to make other players collapse and touch their behinds on the ground. To do this, a player uses his arms or legs to hook the arms or legs of another player. Once another player is hooked, he pulls the other player's arms or legs out from under her. This usually makes a player collapse to the ground.

Note: Watch for someone trying to attack someone else. Then quickly hook her arm or leg away when she is not looking.

Clock Tag

How to Play: Draw a big circle in the sand, and divide it into six parts. One player is "It." She stands in the middle, and the other players stand on the lines of the circle. "It" then has to catch someone by running along the lines after him. All players must stay on the lines. If "It" catches someone or spots someone stepping off the lines, then that person becomes the next "It."

Variation: This game can be played with a variety of shapes. Perhaps start with circles, and then try loops. The only requirement is that the lines have to join at some point so that players don't get trapped at the end of a line.

Note: This game can also be played on a playground. There, children can use chalk to draw the circle.

Beach Burst-Out

How to Play: One person is "It." Two or more players form a circle by joining hands. "It" stands in the middle of the circle and tries to break out by running into the player's hands. "It" tries to run hard enough so that the players are forced to let go of each other's hands. The other players hold hands tightly and try to stop "It."

If "It" breaks out, she is the winner. Then another person takes a turn as "It." Play continues until everyone has had a turn or until players tire of the game.

Any Changes?

How to Play: One person is "It." He sits or stands perfectly still in one position. The other players gather around him and try to memorize everything about the way he looks.

Next, the players look away from "It" or cover their eyes. "It" then changes five small details of his appearance. When he is ready, the other players look at him and try to find the five changed things. When someone believes she has all five changes recognized, she tries to name them. If she is right, she becomes the next "It."

Examples

- Undoing a button
- Changing the position of a hand
- Crossing legs or arms the other way
- Tilting a hat in another direction

Moon Moon

How to Play: Draw a circle in the sand about five steps across. These steps should be by someone of medium height.

One person is the sun. The other players are the moons. The sun has to catch the moons. The moons go inside the circle, and the sun has to stay outside it. The sun has to run around the circle, trying to tag the moons. The sun may lean into the circle as long as she keeps her feet outside. She may even put a hand on the ground in order to reach further inside the circle.

When a moon is caught, he becomes the next sun. If the circle is a bit big, when a sun catches the first moon, she becomes a sun as well. That way, there are two suns trying to catch the moons.

Variation: Divide the circle in half. The sun can now move along the diameter as well as around the circle. The sun is still able to lean and support himself on one hand, but he must keep his feet on the line.

What Do I Hold?

Props: Small objects found on a beach, such as shells or stones

How to Play: One player is the first hider. She goes and finds an object small enough to hide in her hands and returns with it hidden in her fist.

Next, the other players take turns asking her questions about the object. The goal is to try to find out what is the object is. The hider may only answer yes or no. The player who correctly guesses the identity of the object becomes the next hider. He finds and hides the next object.

Examples

- Is it smooth?
- Is it soft?
- Is it green?
- Does it come from the sea?

Note: This game is a natural for the beach. It is useful as a cool-down game after more strenuous tag games.

any size

Beach Games

Hopscotch

Props: Small stone

How to Play: Draw a hopscotch grid in the sand. Make each square big enough for a foot to land in without stepping on a line. Decide whether or not players will receive a second turn if they successfully hop through the scotch.

Players take turns moving through the grid. They stand at the start and throw a stone in one of the boxes. If the stone ends up on a line or goes outside a box, it is the next player's turn. When the stone lands in a box, the player hops up the scotch by putting one foot in a single box and one foot each in the double boxes. They must not step on a line. If they do, it is the next player's turn.

If the player reaches the box where the stone is, she picks it up and puts her initial in the box. Depending on the group's decision before the game began, she may then either have another turn for a successful hop or else it is the next player's turn. The winner is the player who first puts his initial in every box.

any
size

Long Jump

How to Play: Draw a line in the sand. The players assemble a little way back from the line. They then have to run and jump, trying to take off from the line. Draw a line and the player's initial to mark the place where each player landed in the sand. Measure the distance between the starting line and the sand marker to see how far they have jumped. Let players do several practice jumps so they can hone their jumping technique. Then draw a new jump pit and have a final jumping contest. The player who jumps the farthest is the winner.

Note: A good handicapping system is to subtract the length of one foot from the players jumping distance for each year older that a child is. This levels the playing field slightly and encourages players to play against themselves as well as each other.

Beach Games

Races

How to Play: Designate a starting line and a finish line. Clearly explain the rules of the race before beginning the game. Players take places on the starting line. On the leader's signal, the players begin the race. They move as quickly as possible to the finish line. The first player to cross the finish line is the winner.

Variation: There are many possible race variations. Feel free to be creative!

Examples

- Hopping race: Around a course or there and back.
- Backward race: Around a course or there and back.
- Piggyback race: Around a course or there and back.
- Three-legged race: Divide the players into pairs. Tie one leg from each member of the pair together at the ankle.
- Wheelbarrow race: One player holds the legs of another who "walks" on her hands.

- Eyes-closed race: Absolutely hilarious, especially for onlookers! Make sure there aren't any dangerous obstacles on the course before beginning the race.
- Sea race: Players run down to the sea and bring some water back in their hands. Give little ones a head start.

Shadow Tag

How to Play: One person is "It." He has to tag someone else's shadow by standing or stomping on it. The other players avoid having their shadows tagged by ducking and dodging. If "It" stamps on a player's shadow, then that player becomes the next "It." Play continues with the new "It" trying to stamp on someone else's shadow. Play ends when everyone has had a turn being "It" or if players become too tired to continue.

Note: This is a traditional game that many people know. Kids love the game, especially the younger ones.

Beach Games

Rounders

Props: A bat; a soft ball

Step 1
Mark off what represents a batting box and the bases as you would if playing a game of baseball or softball somewhere other than on a baseball diamond.

Step 2
Divide the players into two equal teams with creative names. Toss a coin to see who bats first. Each team appoints a scorer to keep track of their score.

Step 3
The object of the game is to score points by making rounders, or runs, in which a player rounds all the bases and makes it safely to the last base. A team receives one point every time one of its players makes it to the last base and is "home." If a player runs around all the bases in one turn, then the team is rewarded three points for their rounder.

How to Play
The batting team lines up to the side of the "box." The first batter enters the box with the bat.

The pitching team places a person at each base, behind the batter, and anywhere else it may choose. The pitcher then takes the ball and faces the batter.

The pitcher pitches the ball underarm to the batter so that it is not higher than his shoulder and not lower than his knee. If the pitcher does this, it is a "fair ball" and counts; if not, it is a "bad ball" (i.e., a "strike") and must be repeated.

Rules
- Each batter will be pitched up to three "good balls."
- He may hit a "good" or a "bad" ball.
- The batter must run if he hits a "good" ball.
- The batter drops the bat when he runs.
- If there are four bad balls, the batter goes to first base.
- When players run, they must touch each base as they go or else run

around the outside of it. If they wish to stop at a base, they must touch it to be considered on base.

- If a player with a ball in her hand touches a base before a running batter gets there, then the batter is out.
- When a player has left a base, they may not return.
- There can never be more than one player on a base.
- If there is more, then the last player to arrive is out.
- Batters must hit the ball forward, or they are out.
- When a player is out, she goes behind the baseline.
- Players at bases wait for their batter to hit and begin running. Then, they also run themselves.
- When a player makes it to home base, they rejoin the batting lineup.
- If a batter's ball is caught, he is out.
- If a running player is tagged with the ball, she is out.

Play for an agreed time or number of innings. The team with the highest score wins.

Variation: An alternate rule is that if a player is out, the whole team is out.

Note: This classic beach game is very similar to baseball. There are, however, several important differences from baseball, including: a batter isn't out if another player catches the ball before it hits the ground, there is no set number of bases or outs, and a fair ball just has to go forward (within the 180 degree space in front of the batter) rather than forward between the baselines.

Beach Games

Kite Frisbee

Props: A kite; a Frisbee; and a steady breeze

How to Play: The player gets her kite up in the air. Then, she should lower it to about 20 feet off the ground and tie it to something heavy. She then tries to hit the kite with the Frisbee as the kite weaves around in the air. Score a point for each hit.

Note: This game sounds simple but is really quite difficult.

2 or more

Beach Games

Frisbee Golf

Props: A Frisbee

How to Play: Plan a golf course. Decide how many holes it will have; nine is a good number to start with. Make each hole a reasonable distance apart. To make a hole, draw a circle on the sand and number it.

Designate a starting line. From the starting line, the first player throws the Frisbee to the first hole. The other players also take turns throwing. Players have to get the Frisbee in the "hole." The player who lands the Frisbee in the hole in the fewest throws wins that hole. The winner is the player who wins the most holes.

Beach Games

Frisbee Tag

Props: A Frisbee

How to Play: Mark an area in the sand, which can be as large or as small as desired. The game happens inside this shape. Funny shapes, such as curves and pockets, make for an interesting game.

One player is "It" and receives the Frisbee. The remaining players stand inside the shape. "It" must stand outside the shape and throw the Frisbee, trying to hit (not too hard) one of the other players. The players must avoid being hit. They can move around inside the shape but cannot step outside the shape. If the Frisbee hits someone, that player then becomes the next "It." If the Frisbee misses, "It" must continue trying until the Frisbee hits a player.

Note: By putting the limit of the shape on the game, it makes it more equal and fun between differing ages. Faster people cannot run far away. This brings other skills, such as nimbleness and cunning, into play; it also stops players from becoming tired too quickly.

Frisbee Boink

Props: Two Frisbees

How to Play: Give each player a Frisbee. The first player throws her Frisbee as far away as possible. The second player then throws his Frisbee to land somewhere near the first Frisbee but not too near. The aim of the game is to hit the other players' Frisbee first. As the players throw their Frisbees, they become closer and closer. If the first player tries to hit the other's Frisbee, coming close but missing, the second player will most likely be able to hit the first's Frisbee because it is so close.

A player earns one point for every Frisbee she hits. Play continues until a player reaches a predetermined number of points, such as five or ten.

Beach Games

Sand Dune Stalk

Props: A soft ball; some sand dunes

How to Play: Designate an area to be a loosely defined playing field. One person is "It" and has the ball. The other players hide in the playing field. After waiting a little time for the others to hide, "It" creeps around trying to find another player. If she finds another player, she tries to sneak close enough to hit the player with the ball. If she misses, she is still "It." If she hits successfully, then the struck player becomes the new "It." The hiding players continue to creep around in the dunes trying to stay clear of "It" and at the same time keep informed about who the new "It" is.

The game continues until players are too tired to continue.

Note: This game contains the two biggest evolutionary thrills known to the human species—trying to catch someone else and trying to move around without being seen and evade capture.

One Pebble Game

Props: A small stone for each pair of players

How to Play: Players divide into pairs. One player in each pair is the hider and receives a stone. The hider passes his stone from hand to hand, trying to distract the other player's attention. He tries to confuse the other player by pretending to pass the stone when he is not. When the hider is ready, he holds his fists in front of him. The guesser points to the hand she thinks is hiding the stone. The hider instantly opens his hand, revealing what is in it. If the guesser is right, she becomes the new hider. If she is wrong, then the first hider takes another turn concealing the stone. The game can be played very quickly.

Variation: The game can also be played with tally sticks. Every time a player makes three successful hides in a row, he receives one of the other player's tally sticks. Play continues until one player has won all of the other player's tally sticks.

Note: This Native-American guessing game is especially good for younger children. It builds the skills for the larger Bone Game (Game #83).

Pebble Golf

Props: A pebble or small ball for each player

How to Play: First, plan a golf course. Decide how many holes it will have; nine is a good number to start with. Make each hole a reasonable distance apart. The distance can be adjusted longer or shorter depending on the age and skill level of the players. To make a hole, draw a circle on the sand and dig a hole big enough for pebbles or balls to fit into. Number each hole, and mark it with a stick.

Each player chooses a pebble that is about the size of a tennis ball. The pebble can be any shape, but the rounder the better. Players gather at the starting line and take turns throwing or rolling their pebbles or balls toward the first hole. The player who gets her pebble in the hole with the least amount of throws or rolls wins that hole.

The game continues until all the holes have been played. The player who wins the most holes is the winner.

Note: This is a great game on a sandy beach with a good supply of rocks and pebbles.

43

Pebble Pictures

How to Play: Ask the players to gather a variety of objects from the beach. Once they have gathered materials, the game begins.

Create an area for each player. In the area, mark a "picture frame." Make the frame an interesting shape and not too big. If possible, make the frame from pebbles or driftwood to make it more attractive.

Have players make pictures using the materials they have gathered. Perhaps give them a couple of suggestions to jumpstart their creativity. Even better, the leader can show by example and make a picture, too.

Players sign their names in the sand underneath their pictures when they are finished. Leave a little message in the sand for other beach walkers to read as they stop to view this surprise "art gallery."

Note: This game is a good follow-up to Treasure Hunt (Game #22).

Sand Maze

Props: A rake; an object to serve as the "treasure"

How to Play: Show the players the object that will be the "treasure." Players cover their eyes and wait in a designated spot. The leader then takes a rake and leaves, making marks in the sand with the rake as she moves. Make the line twist and turn and zigzag. After the leader is a good distance away, she buries the treasure or hides it well.

At the leader's signal, the players uncover their eyes. They follow the crazy rake marks in the sand to find the treasure.

Sand Figures

Of all the things to do on the beach, building sandcastles is the most obvious and enjoyable. Creating sand figures is an inclusive activity that can involve everyone in the family.

This section provides ideas for different sand figures to make. There are many different types, ranging from traditional sandcastles to complicated sand sculptures. No matter the players' ages or skill levels, there are sand figures that will suit them. Encourage all the players to contribute and use their creativity.

Sand figures can be made as large or small as desired. A dolphin, for example, can be ten inches or four feet long. First, outline the figure in the sand. Then use a shovel or hands to pile enough sand to make the figure.

Next, decorate the sand figure. Players gather materials from the beach and give their creations eyes, teeth, or designs. In a way, it's like making a snowman in the summer!

Note: For perfect sandcastles every time, scoop several shovels of sand into a bucket. Then firmly press the sand into the bucket. Next, fill the rest of the bucket, pat the sand down, turn the bucket over, and tap the outside of the bucket lightly while lifting the bucket straight up.

Things to Bring

- Shovels: it is a good idea to have a few different sizes. To quickly pile up the sand and dig large holes, you need bigger shovels. For filling buckets and patting down, a smaller shovel is ideal.
- A rake: useful for clearing sand away from sand figures and for making "scales" and marks on sand sculptures.
- Buckets of various shapes and sizes: useful for gathering sand and vital for forming castles of different sizes.
- Frisbees

Jaws

Props: Shells; pebbles; other materials to decorate the figure

How to Play: Draw a circular outline in the sand. Pile the sand as high as possible inside the circle. Then all players work together to pat the sand down, making the nose. Sculpt the place where the eyes go. Use shells, white pebbles, or white bottle tops for the eyes.

Mark the mouth, and dig it out, patting the lower jaw firmly as this is done. Then it's time to decorate! Ask players to collect shells or sticks and put the HORRIBLE teeth on the figure!

Note: This shark is so popular that it may be hard to persuade the family to make any of the other figures!

Sand Figures

Seahorse

Props: A shovel

How to Play: Draw the shape in the sand. The head is like a small horse's head, hence the creature's name. Pay special attention to shaping the tail and the spiral.

Next, players pile the sand as high as possible inside the shape. Then they work together to pat the sand down, sculpting the figure. To create the edges, use a shovel to cut "V" shapes that connect to each other.

Note: Don't get too fussy about the details. If the figure develops a slightly different character, explore the group's creativity. Make some fantasy creature instead of a seahorse.

Racing Car

Props: Materials to decorate the figure

How to Play: Draw the shape in the sand. Make the size according to the length of one of the players. He can "drive" the car when the figure is finished.

Now players pile the sand as high as possible inside the shape. Then work together to pat the sand down, sculpting the figure. The younger players form the wheels and decorate the car.

Variation: Dig a seat as well as leg and foot holes into the sand.

Sand Figures

Mermaid

Props: A bucket or empty yogurt container; a stick

How to Play: Draw the shape in the sand. One of the players is the mermaid. This player sits on the shape in the sand. The other players cover her legs and feet with sand, forming it into the mermaid's tail.

Make the scales by scooping a bit of sand with a bucket, empty yogurt cup, or other small container. Draw the fin lines with a stick or fingers.

Note: This one always makes a great photo. Before taking a photograph, rake the sand smooth all around the mermaid to make the figure more noticeable.

Drip Castles

Props: Seaweed; shells; plastic figures (all optional for decorations)

How to Play: A player puts his hand into a pool, stream, or the sea and grabs handfuls of wet sand, placing these mounds close to each other.

To start with, it is good just to quickly drop a few mounds next to each other. On top of these mounds, the player dribbles sand through his fingers. Soon towers and turrets form. The player drips tiny drops of wet sand on the mounds to see how high he can make them.

The results are beautiful. The player decorates his creations with seaweed and shells. Perhaps he even places little model figures inside the castle. The variety and decorations are limited only by the player's imagination!

Note: These castles need wet sand and water. So creating the figure near a pool or a small stream works best. Wet sand is magic stuff. The water runs out of it, and it turns hard. One second it is flowing, the next it is solid.

Outdoor Games

These are games for playing on trips to natural locations or parks. They provide safe, constructive ways for children to discover the wonders of nature. These games are especially suited for adult participation. Most children are capable of learning the games and leading an adult through them.

A play session of several games really helps children experience the landscape and its special features. For example, Camera Kids (Game #50) is a good game to begin a natural adventure. This game goes well with Meet a Tree (Game #52) followed by Duplication (Game #53). Children especially love to have a special tree and will feel a sense of connection with it for a long time afterward. This can be encouraged by return visits to see if your child remembers which was the special tree. The child might even want to bring the tree a present!

Camera Kids

How to Play: The players divide into pairs. One player from each pair is the photographer. The job of the photographer is to take a predetermined number of photographs of beautiful natural features. The other player is the camera.

Before beginning the game, explain how the photographer will go about taking pictures. It is best not to talk during the game itself, so some prearranged signals are useful. A touch on the knees means to kneel down. A touch on the forehead means to tilt the head up slightly; a touch on the chin means to tilt the head down. To move the camera player forward or back, the photographer should apply gentle pressure on the shoulders. Have the players practice the signals. Once the signals are understood, the game can begin. Ask the camera to close her eyes. The photographer leads her gently by the hand until he finds something he wants to "photograph." Let's say the object is a flower. The photographer leads the camera up to the flower and positions her (with her eyes still closed!) six inches to one foot away from the flower.

When the photographer is happy with the position of the camera, he presses down with one finger on her shoulder, and she opens her eyes (the shutter). The photographer counts silently to three and presses the camera's shoulder again. She closes her eyes once more. An image of the beautiful flower will now be photographed inside her mind.

The photographer leads the camera around until he takes about five "photos." Then have the pair sit down, relax, and discuss what they saw.

Examples

- A tree
- A leaf
- Some moss
- A colorful rock
- Any unusual natural feature

Note: This game turns one player into a camera and another into a photographer!

Lost World

Props: A magnifying glass; a piece of string for each player; toothpicks

How to Play: Give each player a magnifying glass and several toothpicks. Place the string in a straight line on the ground. The first player lies down on his stomach with the magnifying glass. He slowly makes his way along the string, looking at all the sights of this wonderful miniature world. He may see tiny pebbles, which look like rocks, perhaps a blade of grass with a drop of water making rainbows in the sunlight, or an ant carrying something back to her nest.

As the player moves along the string, he places the marker toothpicks in places of special interest. Each place he marks is his discovery, and he will be naturally proud to show it to other players.

When the players have finished exploring, ask them questions about what they may have seen. This stretches their imagination and takes them deeper into the world they have just discovered. It also helps them to ask their own questions.

Examples

- Does the ant have many friends?
- What does she eat?
- What happens to a drop of dew?
- What is the name of this world you have found?
- Did you see any little people there?
- What did that slug and the beetle say to each other?
- What did the ground smell like?

In this way, the different worlds of science and fantasy intertwine, enriching each other. This can lead to discussions about how things work, storytelling about the creatures they observed, or drawing pictures of this tiny world.

Variation: Have the player form a circle with the string. She then explores everything inside the string circle...her lost world.

Note: This game provides an ant's eye view of the world. Children love small things, and Lost World helps players observe the micro level of nature.

Outdoor Games

Meet a Tree

Props: A blindfold for each pair of players

How to Play: Designate a starting line. It's best to start at least twenty feet away from the trees. Players divide into pairs. One player is the leader. The other player is blindfolded.

For safety, set guidelines before beginning the game. Make sure the leaders know to be gentle and that they must keep their partners safe from obstacles, such as holes.

Next, play begins. Leaders should guide their blindfolded partners toward the trees. The leaders try to make the blindfolded players lose their sense of direction. To do this, they can lead them gently in one direction, then another, or turn them around. At the signal, each leader guides his partner to a tree and has her wrap her arms around it as best as she can.

Let the blindfolded players hold the trees for a few minutes. Then the leaders ask them to do things to explore the tree with their senses.

Examples
- Rub their cheeks on the bark of the tree
- Feel the bark with their hands

- Smell the tree
- Find branches or knots
- Find things, such as moss, that are growing on the tree
- Feel the shape of the tree's leaves

At a signal, they let go of their tree. The leader guides them back to the starting position, trying again to confuse their sense of direction. The leaders can be creative. They can have fun getting their blindfolded partners to jump imaginary holes or duck under imaginary branches.

When the players are back at the starting line, the blindfolds are removed. The leaders stay at the starting line while the once-blindfolded players use their eyes and senses to go and try and find their tree. When they think they have found their tree, they come back and check with their leader to see if they are correct. Players switch roles; the leader is now blindfolded and vice versa. They then repeat the game.

Note: The location for this game is important. It is best to be near a forest or a group of trees in a park.

Duplication

Props: Objects; a covering, such as a towel, to place over objects

How to Play: The leader secretly gathers about ten objects from the immediate area. These items might be leaves, nuts, berries, stones, or whatever materials are readily available nearby.

To begin the game, the leader lays the objects on the ground and covers them with something. The other players gather around the covered objects. The leader lifts the cover and gives players to the count of thirty to study the objects and attempt to remember them. Then, he covers the objects again.

Players now have ten minutes to explore the area to try and find one of each object.

When time is up, the leader calls them back. They sit in a circle. The leader then removes each object from under the cover, one at a time, with a flourish. He examines each object, drawing attention to any curious features, and passes each one around the circle for all the players to examine. While the players are passing the object, the leader tells them as much as possible about the object and perhaps makes up a little story about what its life might be like. Then he asks if any player has found an object like it. Each player shows their object and talks about where they found it.

Children have great natural curiosity, especially concerning small objects. They will easily become absorbed in the game. The winner is the player who found the most objects, but usually the interest in the finds is reward enough.

When finished, ask the players to replace each object wherever they found it. This tests their memory and tracking skills. It also helps to preserve the environment.

Note: This is a good game for picnics, walks in the park, or a lazy day on the beach. There is some planning ahead involved in this game.

Games to Play at Home

Electronic media can only serve as a partial answer to children's leisure. Sharing games and activities with them helps give them the patterns they need to create their own structures of time. This is most important for children, especially as safety concerns prevent most children from being able to wander freely. Because of this, it is vital that children have creative patterns to use that can exercise, challenge, and inform them.

To help accomplish this important objective, this section of games is designed to keep children occupied when they are at home. The games are perfect for playing during holidays, weekends, or evenings.

One of this book's goals is to encourage the learning of ball skills at an early age at home. Learning this skill encourages physical activity, helps develop motor skills, and increases the interpersonal bond between the family members who play together.

It is from tiny beginnings such as these that great things are built. It would be wonderful if families across the country would go in their backyards and play catch. This activity is especially beneficial for fathers who are displaced from their children. Playing catch is one of the best things fathers can do with their children when they have custody. Never mind the fast food or the expensive present, just put in some time throwing a ball back and forth, and the children will love it.

Disc Jockey Hockey

Props: A kitchen table, preferably round but square is acceptable; four discs per player (quarters or poker chips work well); one "Jack" (old CDs or jam-jar lids work well); a ruler or tape measure for scoring

How to Play: Players divide into two teams. Each player receives four discs and marks them with a colored felt tip of their choice.

Put the large, heavy metal disc, known as the "Jack," in the middle of the table. Players assume positions around the table. Players try to get their discs as close to the Jack as possible. To do this, each player takes a turn putting one of his discs on the edge of the table with part of the disc sticking over the edge. He then bangs the disc with the palm of his open hand, and this sends it shooting across the table. Players can bump into other players' discs and push them out of the way if they can. If a player's disc goes off the edge of the table, it is then dead for that round and scores no points. A round is made up of each player, in turn, shooting a disc at the Jack until all players have used their stock of four discs.

Any player who knocks the Jack off the table loses two points!

At the end of a round, the leader does the scoring. The disc furthest from the Jack gets one point, and the next furthest gets two points, and so on. The closest disc receives double the maximum points.

Play continues for an agreed number of rounds. Then the score is tallied. The highest score is the winner.

Variation: Another way to play is to try to knock the Jack off the table! No score is kept. Players try to bump the Jack off the table with their discs. They have to be careful not to leave the Jack too close to the edge giving other players an easy shot! Discs that go off the table are considered out of play. What works well is to play one way and then the other.

Racing Frogs

Props: One cardboard frog per player; crayons, colored pencils, or markers; string; scissors

How to Play: Cut out as many frogs as there are players. Medium thickness cardboard works well, and each frog should be about five inches across. Punch a hole near the top of each frog's head and thread a six-foot string through each.

Tie one end of each string to a handle or other solid object. A door handle, drawer handle, or back of a chair works well. People can play if the frogs are tied to different handles, but it works best if all are tied to the same handle. Players will have to stand slightly apart and make a "V." This way, players can bring the frogs close together and jockey for position. The more experienced players can create obstructions and perform other dastardly maneuvers.

To begin the race, place each frog at the starting position. At the leader's signal, the players move the frogs down the string by jerking the string. Each player will have her own technique. It's good to allow a few practice runs before racing. When doing the actual race, running commentaries from the leader add to the atmosphere.

Notes

- Make the strings longer for older, more experienced players. This is a natural handicap that will help level the playing field.
- Combine this game with an art project and have the players give the frogs colors and names.

Smaug's Jewels

Props: A blindfold; a few objects to serve as "treasure"

How to Play: Tell the players the story of Smaug. Smaug is a dragon of olden times who jealously guards his treasures. He is older and has gone blind, yet he is still a fearsome dragon whose very touch can turn someone to stone. Using only his ears and senses, Smaug guards his treasures against those who would steal them.

One player is Smaug, the dragon, and he is blindfolded.

Between his feet or knees, place three to five pieces of treasure.

The other players must try to silently creep up on Smaug and steal his treasures without being touched. If Smaug touches them, they are turned to stone and must stand still and silent until the end of the round.

Play continues until all the pieces of treasure are stolen. When the last piece of treasure is successfully taken, then the tagged players are no longer stone. The player who took the last piece becomes Smaug and is blindfolded. A new round begins. If Smaug successfully catches all the would-be robbers, then he is Smaug again. In the next round, though, he must use only one hand.

Notes

- This is a good game to play before bedtime. The tag component tires children out and thus makes them relaxed and ready to listen to a bedtime story.
- This game can also be played on a school playground, on the beach, and in the garden, especially when the children have a few friends to play with.

Sevens

Props: A ball, either a tennis ball or a hard rubber ball

How to Play: Have the player find a wall, preferably with a good flat surface of concrete on the ground. The player stands a comfortable distance from the wall depending on his ability, size, and strength. When a player is starting, nearer the wall is better. The player will soon figure out how to adjust the distance, since he is basically playing against himself. Once he can do it the easy way, he progresses to a greater difficulty level.

Here are the steps a player should follow:

Onesies: Throw the ball against the wall and catch it.

Twosies: Throw the ball against the wall and let it bounce before catching it. Do this twice.

Threesies: Throw the ball against the wall and clap before catching it. Do this three times.

Foursies: Throw the ball against the wall, spin around, and catch it after the first bounce. Do this four times.

Fivesies: Throw the ball against the wall, clap twice behind the back, and catch it. Do this five times.

Sixies: Throw the ball against the wall, bend down and touch the ground, and catch it. Do this six times.

Sevensies: Throw the ball against the wall, clap hands once in front and once behind, and catch it. Do this seven times.

The player passes through the rounds. If the player drops the ball, he has to return to the start and complete the steps over again. The pressure to get it right increases with each round, making the player's focus and attention increase as well.

The player can compete with himself to see how high he gets, which is the easiest, or he can make a scoring system.

Notes

- This is a game for just one player and a wall! It's good to teach a child games she can play on her own as this gives her ways of spending quality time with herself. This game also gives a player the framework for practicing his catching as a skill, which is then a building block for other ball games. In many ways, this game can be seen as the start of all ball games.

- Pet shops are quite a good place to get hard rubber balls as dog owners buy them for their dogs to chase.

Flour Tower

Props: A shallow bowl full of flour; a coin; a board, such as a cutting board; and spoons

How to Play: Fill the bowl with flour, and press it down tightly so that it compacts. Put the breadboard or other board over the bowl and turn both upside down. Lift the bowl so the flower is left standing on the board in the shape of the bowl.

Put a coin in the middle of the mound, and give each of the players a spoon or plastic knife. Players take turns cutting away some flour without disturbing the coin. This is quite easy to start, but it soon gets more difficult as the coin is left standing on a skinny little tower of flour. The player who makes the coin fall loses the game.

Notes
- This is a game for the kitchen. It gives children something to play while waiting for cookies to bake!
- For hygiene, boil the coin in a little water for a few minutes before use.

Pebble Breath Hold

Props: Twenty small objects, such as coins, marbles, pegs, or stones

How to Play: Lay the objects out in a line on the ground that is drawn on the ground or in the sand. If you are indoors, you can perhaps use a line that exists in a rug pattern or you can use a designated floorboard.

A player squats beside the line. When the leader says, "Breathe," the player takes as deep a breath as she possibly can. When the leader says, "Go!" she picks up one object and moves it a short distance to the right. As she does this she says, "Ha! Ha!" She then picks up the next object, moving it a bit to the right while once again saying "Ha! Ha!" She works her way down the line in this way until she runs out of breath, at which point she should stop. If she gets to the bottom and still has air in her lungs, she should start again from the beginning of the line and continue until she is out of breath.

Count the number of objects she has managed to move; this is her score. The next player then takes his turn. Since older players have larger lungs, make them say "Ha! Ha! Ha! Ha!" so they will use up twice as much air each time.

Players can see how they improve by playing a series of rounds. Their performance becomes better as they learn about breath control and how to more effectively manage their energy and the situation.

Note: This is an endurance game for young warriors to help discover their physical limits and to learn to play with them.

Sardines

How to Play: The player designated as the hider goes and hides while the rest of the players cover their eyes and count to a predetermined number. The hider has to hide somewhere where there is room for others to hide as well.

When the count is complete, the other players shout, "Coming," and try to find the hider. When a player finds the hider, she has to hide with him without letting any of the other seekers know. This may involve coming back when the coast is clear.

The game ends when the last player finds the hider (and others who by now are squeezing in together and trying to keep quiet). The first person to find the hider gets to be the new hider in the next round.

Note: This game is a bit like hide and seek in reverse!

Snap

Props: A deck of cards

How to Play: One player is the dealer. The dealer shuffles the cards and deals them equally to all the players. Players do not look at their cards but keep them face down. One player starts the game by laying down a card face up, and the others follow in a clockwise direction.

When one player lays down a card that is the same type as the one before, players must yell "SNAP." The first player to do so, by agreement with all, gets to pick up all the opened cards and add them to her pile. She then lays the first card of the next round and play proceeds. Play continues until one player has all the cards. That player is the winner.

Note: This is the simplest and most classic card game of all time.

Hunt the Slipper

Props: An object to hide

How to Play: The leader selects an object to hide. The bigger the object, the easier it is to find. When playing with young children this is important, hence the use of a slipper. For older children, make the object smaller and harder to find. Show the players the object. One player is the hider.

Next, the other players cover their eyes. The hider goes and hides the object. When the hider is ready, he returns to the other players. At the leader's signal, the players explore and try to find the object. The first player to find the hidden object is the winner. This player becomes the new hider for the next round.

Note: This is mainly an indoor game, but it can also be played outside. Probably one of humankind's oldest games, this game involves hiding an object and letting others look for it. Finding things goes far back into our human history as hunter-gatherers, which may help to explain the deep pleasure and thrill of this game.

Kim's Game

Props: A collection of small objects; a tray; a covering cloth

How to Play: Place a collection of small objects on a tray. Cover the objects with a cloth.

Players gather together in front of the tray. Make sure all of the players can see the tray. Remove the cover, and give players thirty seconds to observe the objects and memorize them. Next, replace the cloth over the objects.

The players now make a list of all the objects on the tray. The one who remembers the most objects is the winner.

Variation: After the objects have been viewed and covered, the players cover their eyes while the leader removes one object. They then view the objects and try to name which object is missing.

Notes

- This memory game, which focuses on the survival skills of memory and observation, is played in most cultures throughout the world.
- This is a good game to help children unwind and focus.

Ban the Word

Props: A chart

How to Play: Make a chart that contains all the players' names. Decide on the forfeit the loser must pay before starting the game. See the Appendix (page 123) for sample forfeits. Choose any common word. Then ban it for the agreed-upon period of time.

Examples

- Go
- Plate
- Down
- Dog
- Yes
- Money
- Bread

Every time a player is caught saying the word or tricked into using it, she has an "X" written next to her name. At the end of the period of time, the player with the fewest Xs is the winner. The player with the most Xs must pay the fun forfeit.

Notes

- This is a piece of pure silliness, which can last as long as desired. A day is fine, but a week is better as it allows for more opportunities to lure other people into making mistakes.
- When playing this game, players should devise strategies for getting the other players to say the word. This requires planning and trickery. Players should also beware of being tricked into saying the word. This means that all the players must find other ways of using words or substitute words for the banned word (e.g., peanut butter sandwich for dog or perhaps hop backward instead of go, etc.). This produces many laughs.

The Search for Alexander's Nose

Props: A fun, unusual object

How to Play: Choose a fun object. This will be Alexander's Nose. One player is the first hider. The hider then places the "Nose" somewhere in the home.

The players continue their normal daily activities until someone accidentally finds the hidden object. This player then gathers all the players together and shows them the object. Players say things like: "So that's where the "Nose" was hiding all the time!" Or perhaps sing some crazy little song that the family has made up to celebrate the finding, etc.

The finder then hides the "Nose" and play continues. The only rule is that the hiding place must be somewhere new each time.

Players become increasingly imaginative in their hiding places because that is where the fun is. Open the umbrella, and, whoops, there's the "Nose"; reach for a tea bag, and there it is; go for a shower, and it's under the towels, etc.

It makes for unexpected laughter and fun whenever someone comes across the "Nose," and it soon becomes a family joke.

Note: This game is called Alexander's Nose because it was first played using a plastic nose from a Groucho Marx mask. Give the chosen object a fun name and perhaps invent some crazy history for it. For example, one family uses a rubber dog bone with stars drawn and stuck on it. They claim that this bone belongs to Spydo (rhymes with fido), their pretend dog who is always moving it around!

Pig

Props: A die; paper and a pen for keeping score

How to Play: Players roll the die to see which player will start. The player who rolls the highest number begins.

The first player rolls the die and makes a note of the score. He then rolls the die again and adds that number to his score as well. He may continue doing this until he *chooses* to stop. Why would anyone choose to stop? If a player throws a one, that is the end of his turn, and he also loses all the points scored in that particular turn.

Play passes from player to player with players keeping their own scores. The more points the player accumulates, the greater the pressure to stop because she just might lose them all on the next throw if she gets a one. The first player to reach a hundred points is the winner.

Note: Pig is the simplest of all dice games.

Birthday Party Games

Birthday parties create special memories in children. To feel confident about putting a birthday party together, it helps to know some good games. Plan to play three to five games during the party. The rest of the time the children can spend time with unorganized play.

A party needs some structure. When the kids arrive, they all need to be involved in something. It is best to begin with energetic games and then some slower games to calm them down before the cake and ice cream. Move things along quickly once the children are paying attention. The first games should be cooperative to build confidence and trust. Follow these with more competitive games, and end with a boisterous finale like Balloon Burst (Game #78).

Charades

How to Play: Choose the title of a film, book, song, play, or TV show without telling the other players what it is. The player chosen to go first has to communicate this title to the others through using mime.

To begin play, the player signifies the category to start with:

- Film: Pretend to look through a camera while cranking it around
- Book: Hold hands together with palms facing upward
- Song: Mime singing
- TV: Draw a square in the air
- Play: Mime stage curtains opening

Indicate the number of words in the title by holding up that number of fingers. The player then mimes each word, not necessarily in order, by holding up the relevant amount of fingers.

The player indicates how many syllables each word contains by holding the right amount of fingers against her forearm. She can mime a syllable if she desires.

If it is easier to mime a word or syllable that sounds like the one in question, she starts by holding one ear. The other players fire guesses, while the miming player encourages or indicates if they are correct.

Signaling that someone has a correct guess is done by touching the nose and pointing at the person who has said the correct word or syllable.

If the word is small like "and" or "but," the player holds out her thumb and forefinger with a small gap. The others then guess.

The word "the" is mimed by holding the first finger across the other to make a "T" shape.

If the player chooses to mime the whole title, she throws her arms wide open.

The player who guesses correctly gets the next turn being the mime.

Variation: This game can also be played with teams.

Note: This game is ideal for playing in the evening with people who are feeling comfortable and relaxed.

2 or more

Flying Fish

Props: Cardboard fish for each player

How to Play: Cut some cardboard fish shapes about six inches long. Have one for each player and a few spares in case of accidents. Designate a starting line and a finish line (usually the other side of the room). Players divide into teams. Players from each team line up behind each other at the starting line. Give each player a fish. Players have to fly their fish to the finish line by throwing it.

The first player from each team flies her fish. If the fish doesn't make it to the finish line, she must fly the fish again until she succeeds. When the fish flies to the finish line, the next player in her team can start. The winning team is the first one to fly all their fish...home.

Variation: Instead of throwing the fish, players can use a stiff piece of paper to fan the air behind the fish in order to propel them toward the finish line (see the illustration above).

Note: The inside front and inside back panels of cereal boxes (the unprinted side) are ideal for making cardboard fish.

Belly Laughs

How to Play: If there are too many children, split them into two groups. The first player lies on his back, and the second player lies down and puts her head on the first player's belly. The third player lies down with his head on the second player's belly, and so on. The last player ends up by the first player, so the first player can put his head on the last players' belly. It makes a kind of zig-zag chain.

When everyone is ready, the first player shouts, "Ha." The second player then shouts, "Ha Ha." The third then shouts, "Ha Ha Ha" and so on. When a player shouts, their belly goes up and down, rocking the next player's head. It is not very long before laughter takes over as they all lie there with their heads going up and down. It's hysterically funny for the children and also to watch.

Note: This game is really good to play just before food is served. It brings the awareness down to the belly and is certainly better to do empty than when the belly is full!

Feather in the Air

Props: A small, fluffy feather or a piece of tissue paper

How to Play: Create a numbered list of simple fun forfeits, suitable to the ages of the children. Players sit or kneel close together. Drop the feather in the air above them. The players blow and flap with their hands to keep the feather floating above them.

If the feather lands on anyone, that player must pay a forfeit. The player on the right of the losing child picks a number, and the child must do the forfeit of that number on the list. Then quickly move to the next round. Play for a predetermined number of rounds or until the players tire of the game.

Examples

- Do a somersault
- Do ten jumping jacks
- Sing a song
- Recite a poem
- Tell a story
- Make a funny face

Variation: A variation is Feather Race, which requires a large room. To start the game, give each of the players a small feather on a plate. Each player has to run to the other end of the room and back. If the feather leaves the plate, the player has to pick it up and return to the start, put the feather back on the plate, and start again. Obviously, the faster the players run, the more likely the feather is to leave the plate! The winner is the first person to get to the finish with the feather still on the plate.

Penny Pinching

Props: Two pennies per player; two wastepaper baskets or buckets or tins of the same size

How to Play: Put the baskets at the other side of the room. Designate a starting line. Give two pennies to each player. Players divide into two teams. Make sure each team knows which basket is theirs.

Teams form lines at the starting line. The first players from each team grip the two pennies between their knees. There is no touching the coin with hands once the race is started. They then race across the room and carefully drop the coins in the basket. If a player drops a coin or doesn't get it in the basket, then he has to pick it up and run back to his team and start again. If a player successfully drops the coins in the basket, she runs back to her team. When she returns, the next player can go.

The first team to get all their coins in the basket is the winner.

Musical Chairs

Props: Recorded music; a chair for every player but one

How to Play: Set up the chairs in a long line or a circle. One person is in charge of the music. The remaining players hold hands. Turn on the music. Players dance around the chairs until the music stops. As soon as it stops, players try to sit down on a chair. Since there is one less chair than players, one person will be eliminated.

Take another chair away and begin the next round. Players dance around until the music stops, then try to sit on a chair. Again one person will be eliminated. Play continues until one person, the winner, is left.

73

Musical Statues

Props: Recorded music

How to Play: Turn on the music, which should be energetic. Players dance to the music. When the music is turned off, players must instantly stand still like statues. They must not move or make any sound or they'll be eliminated from the game. Vary the length of the music so that players do not know what is coming. To begin, have players dancing for a long time and posing as statues for a short time. As the game proceeds, make the dancing time shorter and the statue time longer. The last person left is the winner.

Wink Murder

Props: A deck of cards; a table

How to Play: Players sit around the table. Count the same number of cards as people, and make one of them the Ace of Spades. Remove these cards from the deck and shuffle them. Deal one card to each player. Each player looks at her card without saying anything or showing any emotion. Place the cards back on the table face down.

One person has the Ace of Spades and is...the murderer.

Players sit without talking and look slowly around at each other, making eye contact. The "murderer" kills her victims by winking at them. When a player has been winked at, he must then "die" as quietly or dramatically as he wishes, but making it clear to the others that he is dead. The murderer must manage to wink at her victims without being seen. If any other player sees her, she may be challenged. If a challenge is correct, then a fresh round is started. If incorrect, play continues.

The murderer has won if she kills all the victims! Of course, when the game has only three players left and she winks murder at one of them, she has to get the other one pretty fast before she's challenged.

75

Chocolate Game

Props: A chocolate bar; a plate; a knife; a fork; gloves; a hat; a scarf; dice

How to Play: Players sit in a circle. Put a large bar of chocolate on a plate with a knife and fork in the middle. Next to the chocolate put some gloves, a hat, and a scarf.

Players take turns rolling dice. They soon realize that the quicker they play, the better for them. As soon as someone throws a six, he gets up and puts on the hat, scarf, and gloves. He cuts a square of chocolate with the knife and fork, which he may then eat. He must not touch the chocolate with his hands and must use the fork to get the chocolate into his mouth.

While he is doing this, the other players are taking turns, rolling the dice as fast as they can. As soon as another player rolls a six, she gets up, and the person trying to cut the chocolate must stop and take off the gloves, hat, and scarf, which the next player must put on before trying to cut and eat the chocolate.

Note: With a chocolate bar as an incentive is there any wonder this game gets everyone going?

Ring Game

Props: A long piece of string; a ring

How to Play: Thread the ring onto the string. Keeping the ring on the string, tie the ends of the string together to make a circle. One person is the guesser. The other players take hold of the string with both hands while sitting or standing in a circle. The guesser stands in the middle of the circle with his eyes closed. One player has the ring hidden in her hand.

When the players are ready, the guesser opens his eyes and has to figure out who is holding the ring and in which hand. The other players pass the ring around the circle without the guesser spotting who has it. The players confuse the guesser by distracting him and pretending to make passes so the ring may be safely transferred. When the guesser finds the ring, he changes places with the player who is caught with the ring. Play continues for a predetermined amount of time or until players grow tired of the game.

Note: Use a washer or curtain ring.

In the Manner of the Word

How to Play: One player leaves the room. The other players have to think of a word that describes how an action might take place (e.g., slowly, carefully, wildly, sleepily, quickly, angrily, etc.). Explain that these words are called adverbs. When the adverb is chosen, the player who went outside is called back in.

The player who left the room then has to figure out what the chosen word is. She asks different players to perform an action "as the word describes it." For example, they might ask someone to hop across the room "as the word describes it." If the word was "slowly," then the player would have to hop "slowly" across the room. The guessing player then tries to guess from the actions what the word is. If she is correct, then it is another player's turn to go outside. If she can't guess the word, she has to ask someone else to perform another action "as the word describes it" until she guesses the correct word.

Examples
- Tying your shoelaces
- Cleaning the windows
- Skipping
- Walking
- Setting a table

Note: Simple adverbs are better because they keep the game moving.

Variation: The guesser can ask players questions, which they must answer in a way that's "as the word describes it." Let's say the word chosen was humorously. The player would ask the others in turn any question that came to mind, and they must answer "as the word describes it." In this case, they would have to answer humorously.

Examples
- What did you have for breakfast?
- Where are the nearest shops?
- What is your favorite subject in school?

Birthday Party Games

Balloon Burst

Props: A balloon for each player; string

How to Play: Have a balloon for each player. Tie a two-foot piece of string to each balloon. Then tie one balloon to the ankle of each player.

Players try to burst other players' balloons while trying to protect their balloon from being popped. Softer balloons are more difficult to pop than harder ones, and so are more fun to play with! The winner is the last player left with a balloon.

As a quick finale to the game, all the other players then have to try and burst the winner's balloon.

Paper Drop

Props: A card that is 4 × 9 inches long

How to Play: Players design and decorate the card. Draw lines across the card that are an inch apart. In the bottom space, write the highest score; start with twenty. In the next space, write nineteen and so on until numbers are written to the top of the card. The card is now ready.

To begin play, have a player position her thumb and forefinger horizontally aligned with a small gap between them. The leader inserts the bottom of the card so it is level with the bottom of her fingers. Her fingers must not touch the card to start with.

Next, the leader drops the card. The player has to grip it between her thumb and forefinger. Her score is the number written in the place where she grips the card. The quicker her reaction, the higher she will score. The player with the highest score is the winner.

Sketch Charades

Props: A large pad of paper for sketching; pens or pencils for drawing

How to Play: Players divide into two or more equal teams. Each team decides on its word, which must be two or more syllables long. Each syllable must also have a meaning of its own, either literally or phonetically.

Examples
- Doorstep   Door – step
- Bookstand   Book – stand
- Satellite   Sat – elite
- Postulate   Post – you – late
- Agriculture   Agree – cult – your

Each team thinks of a sketch that illustrates each syllable of the word. They must also think of a sketch that illustrates the whole word.

If the word was "doorstep," then there would be a sketch that contained the syllable "door," and a sketch that contained the syllable "step," and a sketch that contained the whole word…"doorstep."

The first team draws their sketches, and the other team(s) must try and guess the word. The team that gets it right receives a point and is the next to draw the sketches.

Note: Here is a classic game that is very rewarding to play. The kids have to be a little bit older for this one, but it's OK for youngsters to be in a team with older players.

Guess Who

How to Play: One player thinks of either a famous person or a local person, family member, or friend.

The other players then take turns asking questions to try to find out who the person is. The questions can only be answered by "Yes" or "No." A player may ask questions until she gets a "No" answer, then it is the next player's turn.

The game continues until one player has guessed the identity of the person.

Variation: The round can be limited to a set number of "No" answers, say ten or twenty. In this case, if no one guesses who, then the choosing player gets another turn. This puts tension in the game but reinforces counting skills!

Spoon Snatch

Props: Spoons

How to Play: Players divide into pairs. Each pair sits opposite each other with a spoon midway between them. At the leader's signal, they both have to try to snatch the spoon. The winner is the one who gets it, and they put it in their pile. Perhaps start with an odd number of spoons, such as eleven. Play then continues until someone captures all the spoons. Since it is an odd number, there has to be a winner.

Variation: Put several spoons in the middle at one time, either in a line or spaced slightly apart. Players then have to get as many spoons as possible. Once a player has a spoon in her hand, she has to quickly put it behind her back before grabbing for additional spoons. She can only put one spoon behind her back at a time!

Notes
- The game can be played with any kind of small object.
- Players can also make up their own scoring system.
- This game helps develop speedy reaction times.

Birthday Party Games

Bone Game

Props: Two small sticks or other objects to serve as "bones"; ten large tally sticks

How to Play: Players divide into two teams, or tribes. It doesn't matter if the tribes have an unequal number of players, as this doesn't unbalance things.

Teams sit facing each other. Each team places their tally sticks in front of them. The aim of the game is to capture all of the other team's tally sticks.

To determine which team goes first, one player from each team hides a "bone" in one of her hands with much show and trickery. She then presents her hands to a member of the other team, and he has to guess which hand it is in. If he gets it right, he can decide if he wants to start as the "shooting" team or the "hiding" team. If he gets it wrong, the other team decides.

Hiding Team

Two people from this team are the hiders. Each hider has one bone. They hide one bone in one of their hands by making a fist. When they are ready, they both hold out their fists side by side. The fists should be presented in a line, so there will be four in a row.

Shooting Team

This team chooses a shooter, whose job it is to guess which hands the bones are hidden in.

The Play

The hiding team sits with their hiders holding out their four fists containing the bones, and the shooter for the shooting team sits in front of them. The shooter and the hiders are not allowed to speak to each other.

The shooter has to guess which hands the two bones are being held in. There are four possible combinations that the bones may end up being hidden in, and there are four signs that the shooter makes to indicate his guess:

- In the two left hands: Sign this by pointing the fingers of one hand to the left
- In the two right hands: Sign this by pointing the fingers of one hand to the right

- In the two inside hands: Sign this by making a fist
- In the two outside hands: Sign this by opening one hand with the palm held upward

The shooter can test the hiders by making the signs and checking their reactions. While the shooter is testing the hiders, the hiding team can sing songs or chant as a way to raise their spirits and to distract the shooter.

When the shooter has made up his mind, he shouts "Ho!" and makes the sign for where he feels the bones are hidden. The hiders then open their fists and show where the bones are.

Scoring

If the shooter has correctly guessed the position of both bones, then her team takes the bones and two of the hiding team's tally sticks. They then choose two hiders and become the hiding team. The other team then chooses a shooter.

If the shooter's guess has missed both bones, then she has to give the other side two of her team's tally sticks. Her team remains the shooting team for the next round, and she tries to guess where the bones are again.

If the shooter gets one of the bones, then her team takes that bone and gives the other team one of their tally sticks. The two hiders between them hide the remaining bone, and the shooter has to guess again. Each time the shooter guesses incorrectly, her team has to give the hiding team one tally stick. The shooter guesses until she captures the bone.

When the shooter captures both bones, then her team becomes the hiding team for the next round.

Play continues until one team has captured all the tally sticks. They are then the winners.

Variation: A simpler way to play is as follows:
If the shooter gets the two bones at the first try, his team receives a tally stick. For the next round, his team gets to hide the bones.

If the shooter finds one bone, then the other team hides again, and no tallies are given.

If the shooter gets no bones, his team loses a tally, and the hiding team gets to hide again.

Notes

- This is a truly great game. It is found all over the world, but this version is Native American. It was played in families and also between families and tribes. One of its advantages was that the game uses signs so that players did not have to understand other players' languages. A good game between two teams can easily take an hour or more, providing an interesting experience for all.

- The hiders can go into a huddle to hide the bones. When hiding one bone, one person has a bone, and the other has empty hands.
- Small sticks, pebbles, and dried beans or peas work well as the bones. These objects should be small enough to be hidden in the hand. It's good for the bones to be different from the "tally sticks." It's quite good for the tally sticks to be bigger than the beans because this gives them more importance. Substitute stones for sticks or use anything handy. Some people like to make their own set of sticks and bones, perhaps wrapping the objects in a nice piece of material for safekeeping.

Tip It

Props: A coin; a table

How to Play: Players divide into two equal teams. Teams sit on opposite sides of a table. One team is the hiding team, and the other is the shooting team.

Give the coin to the hiding team. The hiding team members all put their hands underneath the table and pass the coin backward and forward to confuse the other team. When they have decided which of their players will hold the coin, they sit still, and the other team calls, "Tip It." The hiding side then forms their hands into fists and brings their fists out above the table. One of these fists, of course, holds the coin.

The shooting team chooses one of its players to be the shooter. The shooter must find the coin. To do this, the shooter calls, "Down." All the hiding players must slam their hands down flat on the table at the same time and keep them there. The player with the coin tries to disguise the sound that the coin makes when it hits the table. The teammates should assist by making loud noises. Shouting isn't allowed, but teammates can slap or bump the table or stomp on the floor as loudly as possible.

The shooter, with the help of her teammates, must decide which hand covers the coin. She chooses one hand at a time. For every wrong hand chosen, the hiding team gets one point. If she chooses the right hand on her first attempt, her team gets a bonus of five points.

The hiding of the coin changes sides each round. Play up to twenty-five points.

Note: This simpler version of the Bone Game (Game #83) comes from the United Kingdom.

Games for Babies and Young Children

Young children up to four years old will be eager to play but won't be able to understand games with complicated instructions. This section includes very simple games specially designed to enhance cognitive development and help the motor skills of these young children. Children find out how the world works through play, and this is an enjoyable experience.

These games also serve as precursors to the more evolved games that children become capable of playing as they grow older. From the beginning, games can cultivate a spirit of fun and family interaction and cooperation. The earlier people start sharing fun and laughter with children, the better. Even babies enjoy a good joke!

Some of the games are so simple that they border on being activities. However, they are appropriate for a child who is just learning about the world. Helping children experience these games for the first time allows them to develop basic skills and creates a bond between child and caregiver.

Many people will be familiar with these simple games, but there will be those who are not. Although simple, these early childhood games serve an important purpose, and they deserve a place in our repertoire.

Play Wrestling

How to Play: Players divide into pairs. Wrestling consists of trying to overpower or outmaneuver the other player in any way possible. So make sure each member of a pair is of similar size and strength.

Before starting the game, establish ground rules. These may include no biting, pinching, scratching, hair pulling, punching, or body hurt. Instruct players that if anyone says "uncle," "enough," or "yield," the wrestling match instantly ends.

Designate a wrestling area. The area should be free from obstacles that could hurt the players. A soft surface works best.

Wrestling partners face each other. On the leader's signal, the match begins. The players move around, trying to be the first to pin each other to the ground. Once pinned on the ground, the pinned player has until the count of three to escape. If he does, the game continues. If he remains pinned, the opposing player receives one point.

Variation: Designate official boundaries for the wrestling match. This could be a mat or chalked lines. Instead of pinning, the goal is to push or otherwise move the opposing player outside of the official boundary. Whichever player does this first gets one point.

Notes
- Play wrestling is as old as the hills. Watch any group of kittens or puppies, and it's virtually all they do. It's the way for animals young and old to test their strength and wits against each other. Boys especially are inclined towards this type of activity. Physical contact is a good and healthy thing for people of both genders. Wrestling can even form the basis for self-defense later in life. Play wrestling helps children learn healthy ways to release aggression and force. It also helps them understand boundaries and physical limits, which are essential to the development of a young child.
- This game can also be played in teams.
- Obviously, adults are stronger than children. If parents are playing, they should use less force and let their children escape and get free.

Try inventing some dramatic persona to make it more fun. For example, I'm known as Shando the Bone Crusher. It's also amusing to give silly names to different wrestling moves and claim that the made-up names are real. For example, "leg scissors" can be named "grip of the python," and one can claim that no one has ever escaped it alive!

Bear Hugs

How to Play: Ask the child if they would like a Bear Hug. If they do, ask them what sort of Bear Hug they would like. There are three kinds of hugs.

First, there is the Teddy Bear Hug, which is light and gentle like a little squeeze. Make a little squeaking sound to accompany the hug.

Second, there is the Brown Bear Hug, which is of medium strength and definitely overpowers the child a bit. Make a low grunt to accompany the hug.

Finally, there is the Grizzly Bear Hug. This is the strongest hug of all, so squeeze as much as the child can stand. Make loud growling noises to accompany the hug.

To play, demonstrate the different hugs for the child. Then ask him again what sort of Bear Hug he would like. Usually, he will start with the Teddy Bear Hug and then work up through the other hugs. Whenever he asks for the Brown Bear Hug, say "Are you really sure?" to build up the tension. For the Grizzly Bear Hug, act worried and say even louder, "I don't know about this. Are you sure? Are you sure that you're sure?" etc.

When the child has had enough of a Brown Bear Hug or Grizzly Bear Hug, she can call out "Teddy Bear Hug." Then the hug reverts back to the gentle Teddy Bear Hugs. Make plenty of noise!

Note: This game is a good one to play before Play Wrestling (Game #85).

87

Flip-Overs

How to Play: An adult and a child should face each other and hold hands. While holding hands, the child puts one foot on the adult's knee, then his other foot on the adult's other leg and proceeds to 'walk up' the adult. All the time the adult must hold his hands tightly so as not to drop him. At the same time, the adult can help by pulling him up if he gets stuck.

When the child's feet reach the adult's chest, the adult helps the child "flip over" in a controlled somersault.

Note: As a safety precaution, make sure the adult can support the child's weight before beginning this game. The game works well only on younger children.

88

Airplane Spin

How to Play: An adult holds the child by the wrist and ankle and lifts the child from the ground. Now gently start to spin around. The faster the spin, the higher the child rises. The adult can "fly" the child up and down.

Notes
- This is a good outdoor game on a grass surface.
- As a safety precaution, make sure the adult can support the child's weight before beginning this game. The game works well only on younger children.
- Watch out for getting dizzy. Make sure to land the child gently.

Whirligigs

How to Play: The child stands with his back to the adult. The adult reaches under the child's arms and locks hands together on his chest. The adult then starts to spin around, letting the child's legs fly out while spinning.

Notes

- As a safety precaution, make sure the adult can support the child's weight before beginning this game. The game works well only on younger children.
- Watch out for getting dizzy. Make sure to land the child gently.

Pattycake

How to Play: One player puts one of her hands down with her palm facing downward. The other player puts his hand on top of her hand with his palm facing downward. The first player then puts her other hand on top of his. He then puts his other hand on top of hers.

Next, the player whose hand is at the bottom of the pile gently pulls her hand out and places it at the top of the pile. Then the next player removes his hand from the bottom and places it on top of the pile, and so on. Do this as quickly as possible. Play continues for as long as the players can continue.

Notes

- This game is a great favorite with most toddlers. Somehow this game rarely loses its appeal and even much older children often still enjoy this game. Getting them to admit their enjoyment might be another thing!
- The game is even more fun with three or more people.

Piggyback Rides

How to Play: The adult bends so that the child can get on his back. The adult holds the child's legs, and the child holds the adult's neck.

The adult can trot around like a horse or simply walk around.

Note: Small children enjoy being higher up and seeing the world from a different angle. Of course, they like being carried as well!

This Little Piggy

How to Play: An adult touches or holds each of the baby's toes in turn, starting with the smallest one. The adult says:

1st toe: This little piggy went to market.
2nd toe: This little piggy stayed home.
3rd toe: This little piggy had roast beef.
4th toe: And this little piggy had none.
5th toe: And this little piggy ran wee wee wee all the way home.

When holding the last toe, as the "wee wee wee" statement is said, tickle the child up the leg and onto the tummy.

Variation: This game can be played with the fingers, too. When holding the last finger, as the "wee wee wee" statement is said, tickle the child up the arm and onto the armpit.

Note: This is a time-honored game with babies and toddlers. It is usually done with the toes but can also be done with the fingers.

Knuckles

How to Play: Both players make fists. They place their fists together so that the knuckles touch. Then the starting player tries to quickly rap the other player's knuckles before she can pull her fists away. If the player succeeds in rapping knuckles, he gets a point. Then he gets to try and rap the other player's knuckles again. If he misses, the other player then takes a turn trying to rap knuckles.

Play continues for a predetermined number of rounds or a set amount of points.

Note: This is a game that develops fast reflexes.

Slip Slap

How to Play: The first player holds her hands about eight inches apart with the palms facing inward. The second player holds one of his hands between the first player's hands. The first player then has to use her hands to try and slap the second player's hand, while the second player tries to avoid being slapped by quickly pulling his hand away.

If the first player succeeds in slapping the second player's hand, she gets a point. Then she gets to try and slap the second player's hand again. If she misses, however, the roles reverse. The second player then tries to slap the first player's hand.

Play continues for a predetermined number of rounds or a set amount of points.

Note: This is another fast-reaction game.

Head over Heels

How to Play: The adult should support the child and assist this movement for the first few times until the child has mastered it.

The child kneels with her head on the ground. An adult knees beside the child to assist. Then, the adult helps the child walk up from the kneeling position and roll over into a somersault.

Notes

- This activity is a fun favorite for younger children. It is perhaps one of the first gymnastic movements, and performing it for the first time never ceases to thrill the proud performer!
- This works well outside on the grass, especially where there is a gentle slope. If inside, consider using pillows to cushion the child's head and protect against falls.

Roly Poly

How to Play: Find a hill with a moderate slope and have the child lie on his side at the top. Next, the child rolls over and moves down the hill by letting gravity do the rest. This results in shrieks of merriment and fun.

Notes

- This game works very well on grassy slopes. Make sure there are no hazards like sudden drops. Also be aware that the children's clothes will probably need a wash after the game.
- An adult should be sitting nearby while the game continues. The adult can help in case of any accidents. Also, the fact that an adult is giving attention is a big encouragement to the children. Shouted comments of approval are also appreciated.

Peek-a-Boo

How to Play: The adult establishes eye contact with the baby, and then covers her face with her hands for a little while. Then she opens her hands suddenly and with a big smile exclaims, "Peek-a-boo!"

Notes

- This is one of the first games most parents play with their babies. It helps the babies learn how to focus.
- The adult should cover her face just long enough for the baby to start to wonder where she has gone. As the baby becomes familiar with the game, the adult can cover her face for longer periods of time.

Touch My Nose

How to Play: Players sit facing each other and look at where the other player's nose is located. Then, the players close their eyes. Next, they gently reach out and try to touch the other person's nose. They may well end up on the other player's forehead or miss the face altogether.

Notes

- This game works well with young children who have some command of their movements.
- An adult can make this game more difficult for himself by starting with his hand further away. This makes it a good challenge for him as well.

Games for Babies and Young Children

Ceiling Touch

How to Play: Ask the child if he wants to "fly up to the ceiling and touch the clouds." If he does, the adult gently picks him up and slowly "flies" him up to the ceiling. Let him touch the ceiling and explore it with his hands for as long as possible before "flying" him back down to the ground.

If the ceiling is low, the adult can hold the child with her back against the ceiling and claim that she is stuck to the ceiling!

Notes

- When a child is small, the ceiling is very far away and feels a bit like another country! This sounds like such a simple thing, but to a small child it is really big and thrilling.
- Be careful to practice safe lifting to prevent back injury.

Donkey Riding

How to Play: The child sits on an adult's knee facing the adult and holding the adult's hands. The adult then starts to sing the following song:

Were you ever in Cardiff Bay
Where the folks all shout Hooray
Did you ever have such fun
As riding on a donkey.

Hey Ho away we go
Donkey riding, donkey riding
Hey Ho away we go
Riding on a donkey

During the first verse, the adult jogs her knees up and down to simulate riding in a mild sort of way. In the second verse, the adult goes really wild and bounces the knees up and down as fast as possible, holding the child's hands tightly. Next, the adult immediately returns to the first verse, and the knee jogging becomes calm again. It's again followed by wild galloping in the second verse. Repeat until tired!

Note: The song can be changed, personalized, or sung however the adult and child desire.

Walking Round the Garden

How to Play: An adult takes the child's hand and holds it open with the palm facing upward. Then the adult places the tip of her forefinger on the palm of the child's hand and slowly makes a circular motion. While continuously repeating the circular motion, the adult says:

Walking round the garden
Like a teddy bear
One step, two step
Tickly under there

The adult should say the first two lines very slowly. When the adult says "one step," she jumps her finger up the child's arm; then at "two step," she jumps her finger even further; and at "tickly under there," she tickles under the child's arm or chin.

Note: As the poem unfolds, the adult should increase the tempo and the volume to build excitement.

Appendix

Sing-Along Suggestions

Good sing-along songs are a valuable asset to any family. To start with, it might be worthwhile writing down the words for most of the songs you like for handy reference. Once you have done this, put these sheets of lyrics in plastic sleeves and keep them in a binder.

For a family song repertoire, choose songs that everyone sings together but also encourage everyone to have their own song or songs. This is a valuable way to instill confidence in people.

Parents have to take the lead with sing-alongs, as kids will learn from the adults. Sing together and to each other so that children will grow up with singing as part of their lives.

Examples
- "Yellow Submarine"
- "I Wanna Be Like You"
- "Michael Row the Boat Ashore"
- "Swing Low, Sweet Chariot"
- "Alouette"
- "Alphabet Song"
- "Ants Go Marching"
- "Baa, Baa Black Sheep"
- "B-I-N-G-O"
- "Old McDonald Had a Farm"
- "Head, Shoulders, Knees, and Toes"
- "Good Morning to You"
- "Do Your Ears Hang Low?"
- "It's a Small World"
- "Twinkle, Twinkle Little Star"
- "Yankee Doodle"

And so on...

Forfeit Suggestions

1. Wiggle your nose and cross your eyes.
2. Tell about a time when you spent a lot of money.

3. Guess how many teeth your brother or sister or you have.
4. Name three things your friends like about you.
5. In a Donald Duck voice, tell Daisy you love her.
6. Make seven animal noises in twenty-five seconds, while someone counts out loud.
7. Say a nursery rhyme while you hold your tongue with your fingers.
8. What's the worst thing you have ever eaten?
9. Blow a bubble using only your spit.
10. Make a funny noise using three parts of your body.
11. Take one shoelace out of your shoe and replace it with eyes closed.
12. Name a silly habit that you have.
13. Name a famous person you think you look like.
14. Touch your nose with your tongue.
15. Tell a short ghost story.
16. Pretend you are asking someone famous for a date.
17. Pretend you are asleep and snore five different ways.
18. Pat your head and rub your tummy for one minute.
19. Say a poem.
20. What's the funniest thing that happened at school?
21. Describe yourself in twenty-six words, with each word beginning with a different letter of the alphabet (e.g., "A" is for artistic).
22. Sing a song while you pretend to play the guitar.
23. Make a face like a fish.
24. Say a tongue twister five times quickly.

Prize Suggestions

For some games, it is fun to have simple prizes. Kids immediately think of money and bought things, but actually it is more enjoyable to have fun gifts from each other. I call this Family Treasure. It can also be used for rewarding a member of the family at home for some particularly great thing they have done.

There are two sorts of Family Treasure. Firstly there are crazy make-believe gifts that can be created on the spur of the moment. Secondly, encourage each member of the family to come up with a small list of services they might like to offer to others.

Ideas for Crazy Gifts

- A magic pebble that can grant three wishes
- A silence stick which, when you touch someone, makes them silent until they are touched by it again
- A feather which, when you put it in a stream, will carry away a fear
- A piece of seaweed that will make someone invisible when she holds it

Family Treasure

- A foot massage
- Cleaning up someone's room
- Singing a favorite song
- Getting something for someone when they are comfortable and don't want to move

Make-Believes

Make-believes are simple games that encourage creativity and imagination.

How to Play: Gather some paper and write one make-believe prompt on each sheet. The prompts can be done individually or given to other players to perform.

Examples

- If the bird of laughter whispered something funny in your ear, what might that be?
- If you could give a gift to a cow in a field, what would it be?
- If you could fly, where would you fly?
- If you opened the lid to the Chest of the Greatest Treasure, what would you find there?
- If you had a wish for each member of your family, what would it be?
- If your TV only played one program, what would it be?
- If you could keep sunshine in a box, when would you bring it out?
- If you had a super power, what would it be?

Tip: Write the same make-believe prompt on several sheets of paper and give them to other players. When the players are done writing their story, collect the papers and read them for the whole group to enjoy.

Storyline Suggestions

Developing storytelling among family members is a valuable skill. This game may be used in the car, at bedtime, or just in quiet moments. Stories don't have to be long to be good. There is a Japanese haiku by Basho that goes:

The old pond—
a frog jumps in,
sound of water.
(Translated by Robert Hass)

Simple is good.

Find out what characters interest the children. For example, they might be very interested in dinosaurs or warriors or eagles. So choose the character, and then just start asking the child questions about the character.

If the story is about a dinosaur, some questions could be:

- How old is the dinosaur?
- Where does it live?
- What does the place where it lives look like?
- Does the dinosaur have a name?

Every story needs a starting point, so the leader begins the story by telling information about the character and what the character is doing. Then some difficulty arises:

- Perhaps the dinosaur loses his football
- Perhaps there is a flood
- Perhaps she is frightened of making loud noises

Ask the child what the difficulty, or problem, might be. They have an astonishing ability to answer the questions.

Once the difficulty is established, discuss how tough it is. Then something happens in the story that solves the difficulty. Ask the child what that something is.

In this way, the story is gently drawn out of your child or children. It will be their very own. The leader simply helps put it into words for them. The child may want to go back to the story again and again. This will create good opportunities to tell the further adventures of Dollop the dinosaur or whoever your character may be.

Not only is this a most beautiful thing to share with the child, but also the child brings himself into the story. This can be a most useful way to gain insights into their emotions.

This is a satisfying bedtime story technique. Most kids will drift into sleep with smiles on their faces and happy hearts.

A different storytelling prompt can be used while on vacation. Imagine the local place as it might have been a thousand years ago. Then work as a family to make up a story about how the people lived then. Think of local people and places and weave them into the storyline. Try creating a fun name for the tribe of people that lived there. There is no need to limit the story by facts: Dragons and other wild creatures could regularly roam through the streets. It's a lot of fun and brings the vacation to life in a different way. It also opens the door to creating pictures and other things to illustrate the story.

Fun Things to Do

There are some things in this life that are important to do. They also feel amazingly good. Here are some things to do that will add to the pleasure of family time:

1. If you climb up a hill, pick up a stone at the bottom and carry it to the top. If there is a cairn (a heap of stones piled up as a memorial or landmark) there, you can add your stones to it. If there is no cairn, then your family can start one!
2. Sit and watch the sunset. Imagine it rising over some other people in the morning and send some good wishes to them.
3. Hug trees.
4. Gather driftwood, and make a small fire in the evening.
5. When you are on top of a hill and there is nobody around, try to make the loudest noise you can, all together. Shout, whoop, and cheer.
6. Throw sticks off a bridge. Every one gets a stick and drops it off one side and then rushes to the other side to see whose comes out first.
7. When walking in front of cliffs, try shouting to get an echo.
8. If you live in a city, try to find walking routes that keep you away from cars.
9. Let other people lead you by the hand while you close your eyes.
10. When you leave a picnic place or your spot on the beach, make a little sculpture, stick some feathers in the ground, or write something in the sand to say thank you to the place.
11. Pile stones on top of each other so that they balance. If you do this by the sea, when the tide comes in, it knocks them over.
12. If you are in a steep valley, watch the sunset, then run up the slope and watch it going down again!
13. Put a message in a bottle, seal it, and throw it in the sea. Write the message at home, seal it in a bottle, and take it with you. Perhaps let the youngest child throw it in the sea.
14. Collect your picnic crumbs and put them near an anthill to give the ants an amazing treat.
15. Arrange pebbles in spirals or hearts.
16. If the weather is very hot and dry, take out a bottle of water and get your kids to choose some plants and give them a drink of water.

Ways to Give Back

Wherever people might travel for vacation, there are ways they can give back to the place and area. There is real satisfaction in this. Letting the children participate in this helps them understand how the world works and helps model the behavior of good citizens.

- Carry old plastic garbage bags, and pick up litter around your family's camp or picnic site.
- If you find litter out in the country, pick it up and deposit it in garbage cans.
- Find some small local charity and give them a donation.
- Write a letter to the local paper to thank the local people for helping you have a fun time.
- Find the local recycling center and use it.
- Go to local flea markets and garage sales.
- Buy local produce.
- Support local arts and crafts people.

Some Good Books to Read

Here are details of some other books about play and parenting that I have found to be valuable over the years.

Steve Biddulph

Steve Biddulph has written some helpful books throughout the years on the subject of parenting. The information in these books is simple to understand, and the books are written in a lively, open manner. His best-known book is *The Secret of Happy Children*. He also has a book of *More Secrets of Happy Children* and a book called *Raising Boys*.

Joseph Cornell

Joseph Cornell is an American whose special area is games that bring us into closer contact with nature. His first book is called *Sharing Nature with Children*, and it contains lovely games that are fun to play and will help children understand how nature works. From this has come the Sharing Nature Foundation (www.sharingnature.com).

Judy Ford

Her main book, *Wonderful Ways to Be a Family*, is full of simple, deep wisdom that addresses different aspects of family life.

The Games Arranged
by Specific Categories

Games for Older Players

  6. Picture Storytelling

  7. Cat's Cradle

14. Spoons

15. Broken Bottles

17. Catch Me Out

18. Waterfall

19. Toe Fencing

24. French Cricket

35. Rounders

36. Kite Frisbee

67. Charades

80. Sketch Charades

Games Requiring Musical Accompaniment

72. Musical Chairs

73. Musical Statues

Games Not Requiring Props

  1. The Farmer Went to Market

  2. Word Tennis

  3. Favorite Dream

  4. Airport Lounge

  5. Family Sing-Along

  6. Picture Storytelling

  8. Blind Distance

  9. Guess the Distance

10. Road Snap

11. Rock, Paper, Scissors

12. I Spy

20. Yes, No

21. One-Word Story

25. Crabs

26. Clock Tag
27. Beach Burst-Out
28. Any Changes?
29. Moon Moon
32. Long Jump
33. Races
34. Shadow Tag
43. Pebble Pictures
50. Camera Kids
60. Sardines
67. Charades
69. Belly Laughs
77. In the Manner of the Word
81. Guess Who
85. Play Wrestling
86. Bear Hugs
87. Flip-Overs
88. Airplane Spin
89. Whirligigs
90. Pattycake
91. Piggyback Rides
92. This Little Piggy
93. Knuckles
94. Slip Slap
95. Head over Heels
96. Roly Poly
97. Peek-a-Boo
98. Touch My Nose
99. Ceiling Touch
100. Donkey Riding
101. Walking Round the Garden

Games in Which Physical Contact Might Be Involved

19. Toe Fencing
24. French Cricket
25. Crabs
26. Clock Tag
27. Beach Burst-Out
29. Moon Moon
38. Frisbee Tag

39. Frisbee Boink

40. Sand Dune Stalk

48. Mermaid

50. Camera Kids

52. Meet a Tree

56. Smaug's Jewels

69. Belly Laughs

78. Balloon Burst

85. Play Wrestling

86. Bear Hugs

87. Flip-Overs

88. Airplane Spin

89. Whirligigs

90. Pattycake

91. Piggyback Rides

92. This Little Piggy

93. Knuckles

94. Slip Slap

95. Head over Heels

98. Touch My Nose

99. Ceiling Touch

100. Donkey Riding

101. Walking Round the Garden